DISUNITED KINGDOM:

HOW WESTMINSTER WON A REFERENDUM BUT LOST SCOTLAND

IAIN MACWHIRTER

Cargo Publishing

To Tiffany, who said Yes even though she said No.

CONTENTS

PREFACE

I started writing this book to record my experiences covering the most extraordinary political campaign I have seen in over a quarter of a century writing about politics. And partly to reassure myself that it really happened. What follows is a personal account: history as I saw it. But I believe it is also an accurate one, based on direct contact with most of the key people involved.

The 2014 independence referendum was a boisterous festival of political participation that brought the highest electoral turnout since the establishment of universal adult suffrage. Nearly half the adult population of Scotland voted for independence in a country that really had no significant independent movement until a decade or so ago.

Of course, the result of the referendum was No, which has left many people in Scotland very disappointed. But I don't believe there is any need to be. The result was fascinating in its ambiguity. The Unionists didn't quite win, and the Yes campaign didn't quite lose.

Everyone accepts that change has to come. The tensions that have emerged between the social democratic aspirations of Scotland and the political realities of Westminster politics are simply too great to be contained within what I will argue is still, essentially, a unitary UK state.

But the people of these islands have been here before and have found imaginative ways of coexisting. The 1707 Union itself was one such, and it worked for over three hundred years. But the paradox of the glorious referendum, as some have called it, is that the old Union became redundant almost soon as Scots had voted for it.

This book isn't a propaganda work, a manifesto, or an attempt to rewrite history. I hope unionists will read it with open minds because some may be surprised at what they find in here. I examine the failings of both sides in the campaign and stress that the real victors were the Scottish people themselves.

As the great Scottish historian Professor Tom Devine said on September 20th 2014 at the Bloody Scotland Conference in Stirling: the United Kingdom state is dead; long live the UK.

CHAPTER ONE

The Glorious Referendum – Scotland's Festival of Politics

A thin grey dawn was breaking over Edinburgh's Salisbury Crags as I arrived at Dynamic Earth, the evolution exhibition in Holyrood, a kind of mini-Millennium dome, for the Yes Scotland campaign's "victory party". It was 6am on the morning of Friday 19th September and there was precious little celebration amid the plastic dinosaurs and luminous planets. The Yes campaign had hoped this venue would symbolise Scotland evolving to the next level. But it didn't happen. For the first time in 300 years, the Scottish people had a democratic vote on whether or not to stay in the United Kingdom, and they voted to remain by a margin of 55% to 45%. It seemed the Great British Brontosaurus wasn't heading for extinction after all.

As nationalist politicians, media figures, and Yes Scotland luminaries milled around waiting for Alex Salmond to deliver the speech they all knew he'd prepared, but hoped he wouldn't have to deliver, there was an air of resignation rather than despair. Many were too exhausted to talk. Of course there were tears – this had been the most emotionally demanding campaign many had seen. The chief executive of the Yes Scotland campaign, Blair Jenkins, wrestled with his emotions as he endured a succession of media interviews asking him "how he felt" about the result. How did they bloody well expect him to feel? He'd spent every waking hour, and most of the non-waking ones too, for 30 months on this campaign – the longest in Scottish political history. He gathered together some platitudes about the great campaign and civic engagement.

The Yes campaign had not been without internal rivalries and policy divisions. Jenkins, a former BBC head of News and Current Affairs, had been accused of spending too much of the campaign's cash on its central Glasgow headquarters and high salaries for staff, most of whom didn't go the distance. But as the morning drizzle fogged the panoramic windows of Dynamic Earth, there were few recriminations. No thumb-over-the-shoulder blaming of others – at least not yet. This was largely because everyone was agreed, even on the Unionist side, that the Yes campaign had been by far the better one – positive, cultural, people-centred and energetic.

Yes Scotland, the umbrella group that brought together thousands of volunteers in 300 local groups, deserved much of the credit for delivering the highest level of voter registration in electoral history: 97%. Mind you, as one guest remarked ruefully, the Yes campaign had been a bit too damn good at generating voter engagement and had inadvertently motivated many Unionist voters to come out and vote No. On the eve of the poll, opinion surveys had forecast a much narrower result: 52% – 48% according Professor John Curtice's poll of polls – which was one reason many believed the Yes campaign had "squeaked it". On the morning of polling day, the media attention had focussed on the queues of eager Yes voters outside the polling stations at 7am. This had left a somewhat misleading impression that the momentum was all with the independence campaign. But the No voters had arrived later, without fanfare, heads bowed, avoiding the attention of cameras and canvassers alike.

No one realised at this stage that Alex Salmond was himself about to be the first casualty of the 2014 referendum night. But there were already suggestions in his short speech accepting the "verdict of the people" that he was part of history. I tweeted a picture of him with the text: "06.20am Alex Salmond's last stand", sensing that he might not be around for long. He certainly looked the worse for wear. The First Minister isn't one to dwell on his defeats however, and he claimed that the result had been "a triumph for democracy" and then congratulated himself for having held the referendum in the first place. And while this was perhaps not the time to say so – even before the formal result of the referendum had been declared – he was right.

The Yes campaign had achieved a very impressive result, even a sensational one. Only six weeks previously, few commentators would have believed it if they'd been told that 45% of Scottish voters were going to vote for independence after an extraordinary campaign in which saw 85% turnout – the highest in any British election since the introduction of universal suffrage. Many unionists had confidently forecast a result of 70/30 in favour of the Union – and with cause. For most of the previous thirty years, one of the abiding constants of Scottish politics has been that only around 30% of Scots consistently tell opinion polls that they want formal independence for Scotland. The vast majority, over 60%, have always said that they wish to see a Scottish parliament with enhanced economic powers – what is usually called "devolution max". So to have persuaded 1.6 million Scots to vote for independence was certainly nothing to be ashamed of. The Yes campaign shook the UK political and financial establishment to its very foundations. It could so easily have been Prime Minister, David Cameron, who was announcing his resignation that morning. He had managed to squander a 22 point opinion poll lead in little over a month. The Union was only saved by a last minute appeal from a humiliated Prime Minister accompanied by the promise from a former Prime Minister, Gordon Brown, of something approximating to federalism.

After Salmond conceded defeat, the Dynamic Earth party quickly dispersed. I said my goodbyes to journalists who had been following this extraordinary campaign, like my old friend from my Westminster days, *The Guardian*'s Pulitzer Prize-winning Ewen MacAskill. Many of the biggest names in political journalism had descended upon Scotland in the previous few weeks and it had seemed as if this little country had become, for a moment, the focus of the world. But not perhaps for much longer. Any way you cut it, the Union had won, and negotiations for Scottish independence, currency, EU membership etc. would not begin later that morning as some had expected. The Chancellor George Osborne did not have to make a speech reassuring the financial markets; the Queen did not have to announce that she accepted the result with sadness; the United States did not have to make contingency plans for the removal of Trident from the River Clyde.

I made my way in the rain past the Scottish Parliament building in Holyrood to the media village that had been erected for the event. I was pretty tired myself, having been up all night doing spots on the BBC's countless election night programmes. But I wasn't downhearted, even though I had voted Yes. I was, anyway, one of the disenfranchised majority who would probably have voted for "devolution max", a form of federalism, had it been on the ballot paper. The UK government had made it a precondition of legalising Scotland's referendum that it was a binary choice: Yes or No. I hadn't really expected the pro-independence campaign to win and I thought this was an impressive result. The Scottish people seemed to have grown measurably in confidence during the campaign.

The tent city in the park next to the Holyrood parliament looked like one of those huge floodlight driving ranges you see in America, only with camera crews instead of golfers; special enclosed pavilions had been erected for the BBC media aristocracy so that they wouldn't have to be exposed to the elements. But the rest of the world's media did it in the cold, with their camera emplacements feeding dozens of satellite trucks. As I climbed up the rickety metal stairs to the Sky News platform, I noticed that the damp precincts outside Holyrood were almost completely empty. Whatever they were doing, the Scots weren't celebrating the saving of the Union. I was there all morning, doing a succession of Unionists-won-but-Britain-will-never-be-the-same interviews, and I saw only one solitary figure appear draped in a union flag, and he left almost as soon as he arrived. Yet, only the previous afternoon I had tweeted pictures of the sizeable crowd that had gathered around Holyrood's ornamental lagoons, including many Catalans flying their colours among the Saltires. Where were all the true believers in the UK? Not even a Better Together victory party. A few early morning souls walking their dogs were ambushed by hand-held camera crews who were roaming the Holyrood precinct looking for reaction. At one point, I noticed a crew doing a piece-to-camera in front of an 'Exit' sign.

This lack of Unionist triumphalism was fitting. It was the silent majority who had come out to the polls to save Britain and they were staying silent. Perhaps they felt they would be accused of being unpatriotic if they celebrated their victory; perhaps they just didn't care. The 2 million who voted No – mainly older, mainly middle-class – were trying to prevent what they believed would be a catastrophic mistake for Scotland. You don't celebrate not falling off a cliff edge. It was only later that we saw one ugly face of Unionist triumphalism when groups of Loyalists bearing union flags and giving Nazi salutes descended on Yes supporters in Glasgow's George Square, ripping up saltires and providing the only serious moment of conflict in the entire campaign. It was all a rather dismal anti-climax, like the weather – a bleak conclusion to a campaign of colour and excitement which by common agreement transformed Scotland and revived the democratic process.

Everyone exposed to the 2014 campaign was changed by it in some way. The sense of political engagement had been palpable on the streets, restaurants, pubs, dinner tables, and bars. This was politics in real time and it was intoxicating. It was a festival of democracy which defied the conventional wisdom of political scientists and opinion pollsters who say that we live in an age of comfort, of political apathy and retail politics. The Scottish people seized control of the democratic process and made it their own.

There was an eruption of political activity in towns and cities across Scotland. The town hall meeting was revived after three decades of decline. In Glasgow's George Square in the days and weeks before the referendum there had been, as one observer put it, "a wee whiff of Tahrir" as thousands of people gathered singing songs, waving flags, and talking politics. The Yes campaign set up a stage and an open mic so that ordinary people, who would never have dreamed of public speaking, talked of their "journey" to the independence cause and their dreams of a better society. It was sometimes naive, but it was optimistic, humane and above all peaceful. This may be a time of political disengagement, of anti-politics, but in the spring and summer of 2014, something different happened in Scotland. I travelled from Shetland to Wigtown; from Stornoway to Aberdeen, and everywhere, I found people talking about politics in the way they usually talk about football and celebrity culture.

I'm certainly no celebrity, writing for a broadsheet newspaper, but somehow my name got around. I found I was being stopped on buses, in supermarkets, in car parks by citizens whose interest in the possibilities and risks of independence was insatiable. I was trapped for half an hour in Sainsbury's checkout once talking about the Bank of England's role as lender of last resort. Some of the customers wondered why it was only banks that seemed to get this free money, and I found that hard to explain. I'd never seen anything like this in my lifetime, and I have been covering politics professionally since 1979 – indeed, I began my professional career as a researcher with the BBC's Referendum Unit for the devolution referendum of that year. That was a somnolent affair by comparison, wholly owned by the political establishment and regarded with thinly veiled contempt by the voters. In 2014, by contrast, people who normally dismissed politics as a vaguely disreputable if not corrupt activity that takes place in the closed precincts of Westminster and Holyrood, were actually living it, as if voting finally made sense to them.

The Yes Scotland campaign had created a network of volunteers across Scotland that was the seed-bed for this flowering of public participation. Using social media and providing local campaigns with funds, merchandising and information, Yes Scotland certainly helped combat the negative messages about independence that were coming from the conventional media. The campaign, under the guidance of its strategist Stephen Noon, a former political adviser to Alex Salmond, was uncompromisingly positive. The aim, as he put it, was "in very personal and subtle ways to nudge, rather than catapult, people to independence". There was an almost evangelical nature to the Yes campaign's talk of "conversion by conversation", building on the late nationalist figurehead Margo MacDonald's call for nationalists to build independence "person-by-person". Sometimes the conversations went on for rather a long time, however, and professional campaigners in the Scottish National Party occasionally despaired of the expenditure of effort on hopeless cases. But you couldn't argue with the commitment.

Some of the optimism and excitement even spread to England and the rest of the UK. The singer Billy Bragg became a regular visitor to Scotland, hoping that some of the radicalism of the independence movement would infect England. Cities and regions started demanding greater autonomy, and a rebalancing of Britain to counter the over-centralisaton of political, economic and cultural life in the city state of London. The First Minister of Wales, Carwyn Jones, declared on the day of the referendum that "the old Union is dead" and demanded a new constitutional settlement.[1] *The Guardian* writer Jonathan Freedland described the Scottish referendum as another "Glorious Revolution" that could transform and revive the constitution of the entire UK, perhaps as profoundly as the original had in 1688.[2] The democratic revolution in Scotland would, English reformers hoped, drive out the lingering vestiges of absolutist centralism from Westminster by reforming the Lords, disaggregating the Commons along regional lines, and reforming the voting system. This was a tall order, however, given the conservatism and inertia of the Westminster political establishment.

INTIMATIONS OF INTIMATION

Writers and journalists like myself often flatter themselves by exaggerating the significance of the political events in which they may have played a peripheral role. Of course, politicians always say they fought the best campaign, and only lost because of dirty tricks and negative campaigning by their opponents. There are many who did not agree that the 2014 independence referendum was so glorious and transformative. The nationalists lost, didn't they? Weren't there also bitter antagonisms and even roots of racism beneath the thousand flowers blooming?

Some newspapers saw a very different referendum campaign, one that was marked by tales of intimidation and threats; of families divided, even of anti-English hostilities. Headlines such as this in the *Daily Mail* on the day before the referendum vote (17/9/14) were not untypical: "Vote yes, or else!: Police out in force at polls as Salmond's bullies are accused of intimidating voters – and even punching a blind man in the face for just saying 'No'." The Labour MP Jim Murphy said he had to cancel his '100 towns, 100 days' speaking tour because he was pursued by "organised gangs of Yes thugs". The activities of the so-called "cybernats" – nationalists making abusive remarks about prominent Unionists like the novelist JK Rowling – were widely condemned. Alex Salmond was portrayed as a deluded dictator of a would-be banana republic.

A new narrative is being written post-referendum in which the excitement and popular engagement is seen largely as journalistic hype and the campaign merely nationalist froth on the cold coffee of Scottish unionism. But I hope this book confirms that in the spring and summer of 2014 something significant really did take place in Scotland, and that even many conservatives and non-nationalists found themselves surprisingly moved by it. While the front pages told of a referendum of hate, in the comment pages a significant number of Unionist writers told a different story. It would be wrong of me simply to assert this and leave it there. So here, in their own words, is a selection of the kind of writing that the referendum inspired even in its critics.

John McTernan, the former Tony Blair policy adviser, and one of the most acerbic and hostile critics of nationalism in British journalism, said in *The Scotsman* at the height of the campaign:

If you love politics then you have to love the referendum campaign. It has spread conversations about politics everywhere – from pubs to offices, to school gates and hen nights. We've seen old forms of communications revived – think of Jim Murphy's epic revival of street corner meetings, 100 meetings in 100 towns. And we've seen new forms, particularly social media, used – and sometimes abused... The hallmark of the debate, despite a few nastier notes in the margins, has been respect, and above all else, seriousness. (23/8/14)

The prolific conservative blogger Alex Massie was equally enthusiastic in *The Spectator*:

From Brora to Ecclefechan, Coupar Angus to Tobermory, this is a time of great and energetic disputation... The referendum is inescapable. Something is happening and that something is important... Yessers and Nawers in Scotland agree on little, save perhaps this: the campaign has been a steroid injection for democracy. Not just because tens of thousands have returned to the electoral register but because politicians are talking about big things at last. Things that go beyond a simple 'yes' or 'no' vote... 'Yes' or 'No', change is coming. This is what politics is supposed to be about; this is what we're supposed to want. (4/9/14)

One of the surprises of the referendum was the discovery that, while many of Scotland's leading authors, like the novelist William McIlvanney, turned to the independence cause, some of the best political journalism came from Unionists. Hugo Rifkind wrote a much-quoted feature in *The Times* on 2/9/13 in which he advised UK readers:

Don't be fooled by the ugliness you've seen on the front of newspapers, or the eggs, or the cybernat ghouls. Rarely can there have been a political battle with such high stakes that has been conducted so peacefully... There are now so many Yes badges in circulation that campaigners joke that, if a currency union doesn't work out, Scotland can use those instead. There are more Yes badges on jackets, more Yes posters in windows, more Yes stickers on cars. Over the past few weeks I've seen the word Yes on hillsides, in fields and on an island in a Hebridean loch. Word has it there's a series of No banners on the A9 north of Perth but I haven't seen it myself.

He went on:

Yes has had a carnival these past two years; a celebration. No has fought hard on "could we?" and probably even won on "should we?" Yet on the great soulful battleground of "all other things being equal, though, would you ultimately like to?" it has not so much been trounced as refused to properly fight at all.

Like many journalists who descended on the referendum campaign, *The Guardian*'s Libby Brooks found she had to confront some of her own prejudices:

I met a woman whose teeth told me all I thought I needed to know about her. Barely past her 20s but already the mother of five young children, she was standing outside a branch of Greggs, waiting for her boyfriend to fetch sausage rolls. She told me that she had registered to vote, having never done so before, and that she supported independence. When I asked why, she said she thought Scotland could do better under a Holyrood government that was more in touch with the country's needs. She added, casually: 'And of course I've read the White Paper.' All my crappy preconceptions puddled at my feet.

Of course, not everyone found the campaign quite so edifying. *The Economist*'s Bagehot column was equally gobsmacked by the referendum, but not in a good way. Under a column headlined: "How A Nation Went Mad", its anonymous author recounted a Yes meeting in a Kirkcaldy church.

A giant Saltire had been projected onto the altar, where the father of Gordon Brown, the local MP and former Labour prime minister, had once preached. Mainly to annoy Mr Brown, the church had been hired by Yes Scotland campaigners to host Tariq Ali, a left-wing firebrand

and an enthusiast for Scottish independence. As Mr Ali entered the church, a lone piper played 'Amazing Grace' at its door. (13/9/2014)

Bagehot condemned the "reckless half truths and untruths" of the Yes campaign, but even he had to concede that "separatist euphoria was sweeping Scotland", reaching parts that Better Together's "project fear" could not. He feared for the fate of the UK:

> This is the lunatic atmosphere into which the Unionist leaders, David Cameron, Ed Miliband and Nick Clegg, launched their humiliating and belated mission to save Britain this week. In the circumstances, it is all they can do. It may not be enough.

In the end, of course, it was enough. As Wellington said at Waterloo, it was a damned near thing – the nearest run thing you ever saw in your life. The Yes campaign made a big noise, but the Unionists claimed a decisive victory. This was not Quebec where, in 1995, the outcome had been so close no one felt they could claim truly to have won. Nevertheless, if only 5% of the Scottish voters had been persuaded the other way, the Union would have been finished there and then. And the aftermath of the referendum campaign has almost been as extraordinary as the prelude to it.

After electoral setbacks, most political organisations descend into a period of introspection, division and decline. But the independence campaign seems to have actually grown in strength: since the referendum The Scottish National Party has more than tripled its membership to 84,000 at the time of writing, making it the third largest political party in the UK. Other independence-supporting parties like the Greens and the Scottish Socialist Party found that their memberships quadrupled.

Holyrood may have been empty on the morning after the referendum, but in subsequent weekends thousands of people staged demonstrations outside the Scottish Parliament under banners like "Hope over Fear" and "Voice of the People". Numerous continuing independence campaigns like The 45, Yes Alliance, Women for Independence, the Common Weal, Radical Independence, the Independence Convention and National Collective have kept the spirit of the referendum alive by holding conferences and street events attracting large numbers of people.

When the incoming leader of the SNP, Nicola Sturgeon, launched a countrywide tour in late October, she sold out Scotland's biggest performance venue, the 12,000 capacity Glasgow Hydro, in 24 hours.

Meanwhile, in a bizarre reversal of roles, the Unionist parties have lapsed into acrimonious divisions and even, in the case of the Scottish Labour Party, virtual civil war. First, Labour and the Conservatives – the key partners in the Better Together campaign – fell out after David Cameron insisted on the day after the referendum that legislation for English Votes for English Laws (EVEL) had to proceed "in tandem" with further devolution of powers to Scotland. Then, on 21st October, the leader of the Scottish Labour Party, Johann Lamont, resigned, claiming that the Scottish party was being treated as a "branch office" by Labour in London. A raft of former Labour ministers echoed Lamont's complaint, which will hang over the party for years after the 2014 referendum, if only because it echoes what the SNP had been saying for years before it.

The Yes Scotland campaign is no more, its head office dispersed, but the networks it created continue, as do most of the Yes groups. The debate has shifted from achieving formal independence to acquiring devolution max, or home rule, at least in the short term. According to the poll of polls, recorded by Professor John Curtice in "What Scotland Thinks" (30/9/14), a substantial majority of Scots want to see control of all important tax decisions devolved to the Scottish parliament, and most welfare decisions also. A clear majority want broadcasting, and other matters currently reserved to Westminster, repatriated. The "settled will" of Scottish voters is to see something that would amount to a qualitative change in Scotland's position in the UK. Westminster would retain responsibility only for defence, foreign affairs, currency and matters like bank regulation which have to be organised at a UK level.

TROUBLE AT THE TOP

It wasn't all positivity within the Yes Scotland headquarters in Hope Street, Glasgow. The former BBC executive, Blair Jenkins, had never run a political campaign like this before and while he was a very effective spokesman for the campaign, able to speak convincingly on TV to middle-class voters, the organisation left much to be desired. In little over a year, the five well paid 'executive directors' recruited by Jenkins in 2012, like the former director of communications at the Scottish Executive, Susan Stewart, had been sacked or left under variously darkening clouds.[3] The only "nudging" that seemed to be going on was nudging people out the door. As one insider put it, "it was poisonous, worse than the BBC, worse than anything you can think of". Indeed, the way some senior Yes campaign figures talked about life at its HQ was like something dreamed up by Armando Iannucci – 2012 meets *The Thick of It* – only without a Malcolm Tucker to knock heads together and make something work.

I also heard activists complain of what one called "top down, almost dictatorial" control-freakery from the Scottish Government. Many felt that the campaign was not permitted a proper say on policies like currency or the EU by SNP political minders and that the overall campaign was too dominated by the personality of Alex Salmond, which for many women voters was a complete turn off. Unsurprisingly, the SNP saw things rather differently. They regarded Yes Scotland as a dysfunctional organisation at war with itself which, in the first year, did nothing very much except burn through a great deal of money – it was largely funded by a £2.5 million donation from the Euromillions Lottery winners, Colin and Chris Weir, who were SNP members.[4] The Scottish National Party tried to turn Yes Scotland into a more conventional political campaign, but that never quite worked either. No one really seemed in charge. Even the computerised canvassing app, Yesmo, supposedly based on the most advanced American campaign tech, didn't work according to many who used it. The root of the problem was that it was never entirely clear how Yes Scotland was supposed to relate to the SNP – as a front or an autonomous body – and, in the end, the party largely took it over, moving in its own people, like the unflappable Kevin Pringle, Alex Salmond's former press spokesman.

The Unionists ran a conventional political campaign, exploiting support in the press and using the Labour Party machinery to get out the vote. The director of Better Together, Blair McDougall, was a seasoned Labour Party insider and had run David Miliband's (unsuccessful) leadership campaign. He was never particularly bothered by accusations that Better Together was too negative. He didn't go in for positive campaigns and stuck to the simple message of what became known as "Project Fear" – a relentless assault on the risk factor in the independence prospectus. Better Together, the umbrella Unionist campaign that brought together Labour, the Conservatives and the Liberal Democrats, appealed to the anxious underbelly of Scotland: the middle-class Scots who worried about where their money was going to come from if England took away the pound. They did this very effectively. The opinion polls indicated that Yes support came predominantly from working-class areas in cities like Glasgow, and also from younger voters. No voters tended to be older (73% of over 65s voted No), female (marginally) and home-owners.

Many reluctant No voters were confirmed in their constitutional conservatism by a last-minute barn-storming speaking tour by the former Labour Prime Minister, Gordon Brown, who may be a discredited figure in England but commands considerable respect in Scotland. He had seized the campaign in its dying weeks and, through force of personality, compelled the three Unionist party leaders to sign a solemn and binding "Vow" – photoshopped in cod vellum on the front page of the mass circulation *Daily Record* three days before the vote – in which they promised "extensive new powers" for the Scottish parliament, no cuts to the Barnett Formula public spending allocations and guarantees on funding the NHS. Gordon Brown had channelled the Victorian Liberal Prime Minister William Gladstone and promised nothing short of "home rule" for Scotland. His key speech was even in Midlothian, focus of Gladstone's own campaign over a century ago. The glorious referendum brought Gordon Brown back from the political undead. Up to 25% of No voters, according to Lord Ashcroft's post-referendum poll, made their decision on the basis of the prospect of more powers for Holyrood.[5]

Many journalists I have spoken to, including ones sympathetic to the cause of independence, have told me that they found the Better Together campaign to be vastly superior to Yes, not only in the stories it managed to place in the media but also on the help it gave to journalists seeking access to senior Unionists and to the campaign on the ground. Many thought Yes Scotland's responses on the currency issue were unconvincing and half-hearted. Editors found they were getting stories they could not ignore from bodies like the Institute for Fiscal Studies and big firms like BP and Standard Life and just didn't get a comparable flow of stories from the independence side. The campaign was also poor at rebutting misleading stories and deconstructing media stunts. The Labour MP Jim Murphy, for example, produced a video compilation of alleged harassment from Yes campaigners during his speaking tour, during which he was hit by an egg. This video-nasty was simply spliced together from camera phone footage of rowdy hecklers and did not justify Murphy's claim of an "organised campaign of mob intimidation by Yes Scotland". The egg wasn't even thrown by a Yes campaigner, and it is clear even from Murphy's video that those holding Yes placards did not support the assault. In another scene, a press photographer is clearly shown trying to incite one of the protesters to hit him in front of *The Times* journalist Mike Wade.

Yes Scotland seemed unable to deal with this crude propaganda exercise, or make clear that Yes speakers, like Jim Sillars, had received very similar treatment on the streets and that there had been assaults on Yes campaigners. The story of Yes intimidation ran for days, colouring voters' attitudes to independence. There were numerous similar examples of this failure to engage. One suggestion was that the Yes campaign felt that it should not get its hands dirty trying to rebut damaging stories. If you wrestle with a pig you both get dirty, as I heard one campaigner remark. But sometimes, unfortunately, you do have to deal with negative stories on their own terms. The Jim Murphy episode was highly damaging because it allowed Better Together to play to the narrative that Scottish nationalists are essentially street thugs of the far right.

AWAKENING

So, almost everything that could go wrong with the Yes Campaign organisation probably did go wrong. Except for one thing: it was actually very successful at what it set out to achieve. By some mysterious alchemy, this dysfunctional campaign converted 1.6 million sceptical Scots to the cause of independence in a country where political nationalism has been largely non-existent in modern times. It achieved this without resort to militant action, ideological uniformity, democratic centralism, agitational propaganda, or demonisation of its adversaries. The hands-off approach perhaps made a virtue out of necessity – but it worked.

Jenkins and Noon got the spirit of the campaign right, even if the administration was chaotic. In many ways, this book is an attempt to find out why it went so right when so many things went wrong.

The campaign on the ground rapidly generated its own formidable momentum as the local groups attracted over 100,000 people into politics who would never have joined a political party. The groups were allowed to do more or less what they wanted: set up stalls, cafes, book groups, community projects. Parallel organisations to Yes Scotland carried the message into various defined areas of Scottish public life, like Women for Independence, Farmers for Independence and Generation Yes. Unfortunately, there wasn't a Pensioners or Seniors for Yes, which might have countered fears, encouraged by Better Together, that voting Yes meant losing pension security. These spin-offs were called "SNP fronts" by the Unionists, and most were initially sponsored and some financed by the Yes campaign, but they undoubtedly took on an independent life of their own – they had to.

In addition to the local groups, new organisations emerged like the Radical Independence Campaign. This federation of left-wing groups and Green Party activists was largely autonomous of the Yes Campaign, self-financing and focussed its attention on housing estates or "schemes" where Labour reigned supreme. In one weekend alone (18/8/14), RIC doorstepped 18,000 voters in 90 working-class communities across Scotland. It discovered that almost two-thirds were minded to support independence. RIC's approach identified potential support for independence that had gone under the radar of conventional polling, in part because many of the people canvassed had never voted before. Apathy and disengagement rather suited old school Labour MPs in constituencies where votes were traditionally weighed rather than counted. In RIC, the various splinters on the Scottish far left discovered the virtues of working together instead of fighting each other. They also discovered that for the first time in modern history people started to listen them.

The left used to talk patronisingly of "educating" the masses, but you realise that in transformative moments like this the people educate themselves. They are much more intelligent than either the politicians or the press think they are. People were asking the difficult questions. Should Scotland set up its own currency, like Norway or Panama, or stick with the UK pound? What should Scotland's relationship be to the European Union, and was the

Yes campaign right to endorse Brussels uncritically? Why was Alex Salmond such a smug so-and-so? Actually, the people were addressing a lot of the questions the Yes Campaign under SNP direction was avoiding and perhaps it should have listened more closely. This was especially the case in working-class areas of middle-class cities like Edinburgh, where people not only embraced the cause of social justice, but started telling politicians how they should set about delivering it – for example, by telling George Osborne and his banking friends that they were welcome to leave Scotland and take their pound with them.

As late as the beginning of August 2014, it had seemed as if the No camp were coasting to victory. But complacency blew up in their faces as their commanding poll lead simply disappeared within the space of four weeks, leaving the Yes campaign briefly in the lead. For one intense moment, the referendum looked as if it might just turn into a replay of the 2011 Scottish parliamentary election campaign when the Scottish National Party, under Alex Salmond's leadership, had come from 10 points behind to a landslide victory in the space of three and a half weeks. (The BBC's Laura Kuenssberg tweeted later that she had been told that a second poll commissioned by the UK government but not published, had shown Yes in the lead by 53% to 47%). Pollsters were confounded, including the US election guru Nate Silver, who had been reported as having said that a victory for Yes was a statistical impossibility (he now claims he did not make such a sweeping forecast). The Yes campaign's advance caused the UK political establishment to dissolve in panic like Lance Corporal Jones in *Dad's Army* – a sight that gladdened the hearts of Scots, whichever way they voted.

Why had the polls moved so dramatically only in the final six weeks of the longest campaign ever staged in Scotland? Well, I think this was probably because the polls had failed to detect what was really happening in the undergrowth of Scottish politics. Unlike in a parliamentary election, where most people know their political allegiances before the campaign begins, in this referendum the people of Scotland had been conducting an open-minded debate for two years and many did not make up their minds until late in the day. But while they were thinking, and for the sake of something to say, many voters told pollsters that, well, they didn't want to break up Britain or anything irresponsible like that. It was a holding position. And in truth, they didn't:

even many who voted Yes believed they could still call themselves British.

In the end, it wasn't leaders, parties, organisation and propaganda that made the Yes campaign such a success, but the Scottish people themselves. Not just the many artists, writers, intellectuals and performers who came together in groups like National Collective to paint a picture of a better nation. More often, it was people living on the edge of society, on the margins of poverty, people who had a lot to lose. Council tenants in the working-class areas of Dundee, Glasgow, North Lanarkshire knew that by participating in this democratic process, and registering to vote, they risked being traced for debts by bailiffs and sheriff officers. And these fears were to prove well founded after polling day as no fewer than eleven Scottish councils, many Labour, used the enhanced electoral rolls – in my view, shamefully – to pursue voters for unpaid poll tax debts dating back from over 20 years – debts that had been long since written off in England.

But these working-class people participated nevertheless, like the pensioner I met in Meadowbank voting for the first time in his life, because for once they thought that they could change something by creating a new society in a new Scotland. This was what made the referendum such an inspiration. The independence-supporting writer Irvine Welsh put it like this: "Forget Bannockburn or the Scottish Enlightenment, the Scots have just reinvented and re-established the idea of true democracy. This glorious failure might also, paradoxically, be their finest hour".

WHERE ARE WE NOW?

This book does not deal with the lead up to the battlegrounds of this vote, the historical path Scotland walked to reach a constitutional referendum. I cover this extensively in my previous book *Road To Referendum* (Cargo). Instead, the focus is on the here and now; the earthquake this vote created and the fault lines it has left in the very fabric of the United Kingdom. I examine the various visions of where the future may lie and ways the Union could stay united in an uneasy partnership rather than full divorce. But the conclusions that we can draw from this turbulent and infectiously exciting time in UK politics may not make happy reading for supporters of the Union.

The thesis of this book is that, while constitutional optimists like Jonathan Freedland are right and that the unitary United Kingdom as we understand it is all but finished, it could still take a long time to die. And in the' meantime the Scottish Question remains unanswered by the referendum. The Union won at best a Pyrrhic victory in September 2014 and unless there is a very rapid, fully federal transformation of the UK another referendum in the next decade or so will assuredly lead Scotland out of it. The aftermath of the referendum, almost as much as the result itself, showed that Scotland has changed in the course of the past couple of years, building as if from nowhere a powerful independence movement unprecedented in modern Scottish history.

In forthcoming chapters, this book will explore the role that culture played in the referendum campaign and ask whether the contribution made by artists, writers and performers was as significant as has been claimed. I believe that one of the reasons the Yes campaign generated such momentum since the referendum is because it dealt, not just in fact and statistics, but in vision and emotion – the stuff of literature and theatre. I argue that groups like National Collective not only lent colour and vibrancy to the campaign, they helped communicate the independence message to a wide group of people who are normally resistant to conventional political discourse.

I also examine the day-by-day coverage of the campaign by the Scottish and UK press, which aroused such resentment among independence supporters. Using data compiled by the independent PR agency, Press Data, it appears that No-supporting stories tended to dominate by around three to one, and nearly four to one when it came to front page leads. It is hard not to come to the conclusion that the press, perhaps unconsciously, became an arm of the Better Together campaign. Social media was only able to mitigate this negativity, not balance it. This raises questions about how referendums can be conducted fairly when there is a lack of press diversity.

The Yes campaign was dogged by accusation and innuendo that it was concealing a nationalism of the far right. I argue that the Scottish independence campaign was a progressive force, like the civic nationalist movements of central Europe in the 1990s. It showed none of the ethnic supremacism or anti-English racialism that many commentators warned would be unleashed by the referendum campaign. Nationalism in Scotland has shown itself capable of mobilising progressive forces for change in a way the Marxist and non-Marxist left has not been able to do for half a century. It is now imperative that this broad decentralised movement finds new non-sectarian structures to keep this civic engagement fresh and alive. The Yes Scotland campaign ceased to exist on 19th September; a grass roots home rule movement must fill the vacuum. It should not merely be collapsed into the Scottish National Party.

In the referendum campaign there were broad hints from Unionist politicians and commentators that, since the UK is evolving in the direction of a federal state, nationalism was redundant. I explore the various interpretations of the *Daily Record* "Vow" and ask whether there is any serious prospect of a federal reconstitution of the UK. Of course, federalism is difficult to establish in a country where 85% of the population live in one part of it, and I argue there is little sign that Westminster is serious about it. Nor is there much prospect of "devolution max", the preferred option of most Scots, whereby Scotland's parliament would take responsibility for taxation and welfare, leaving defence, foreign affairs, and macro-economic management with Westminster. This has also been ruled out by the Unionist parties, on the grounds that it is "independence by another name".

This apparent rejection of federalism is one reason why the former leader of the SNP, Alex Salmond, is so confident that victory for independence is only a matter of time. The SNP is likely to be an important force in UK politics for the foreseeable future, despite the referendum setback. The party is more popular than ever, topping 40% in the post-referendum polls. Salmond dominated the independence movement for 25 years and has now handed over to his deputy, Nicola Sturgeon, who is an impressive politician and a worthy successor. However, I make clear that Salmond is a hard act to follow and that Sturgeon's honeymoon with the press has been short-lived. Alex Salmond was Scotland's first truly national political leader. And as he made the Scottish Parliament believe in itself he helped the Scottish nation re-discover itself

To her credit, Ms Sturgeon did not boycott the Smith Commission on further devolution or wish it to fail to foment grievance. However, that grievance will foment itself if the UK does not heed the lesson of the referendum and seek major reform. There are many angry and discontented people in Scotland,

and while the Scottish referendum campaign was peaceful, its aftermath may not be. Scotland can be justifiably proud of a campaign that was meticulously democratic and peaceful – with not a pane of glass or a punch thrown in the cause of independence. The solitary egg, hurled at the Labour MP Jim Murphy, the future leader of the Scottish Labour Party, was the exception that proved the rule.

The Scots are not revolutionary people – they have seen in their own violent history the damage that can be caused by the politics of the rush of blood to the head. Scotland is an old country and its people know that when they antagonise their larger neighbour they generally come off worst, whether on the battlefield or on the currency markets. They are, after all, as the writer Ludovic Kennedy said, "in bed with an elephant", and you have to think carefully before you risk poking it. Scots had been given a very serious warning from the Westminster political establishment that if they voted Yes they would lose the financial security of retaining the pound. However, this very policy, while it may have won the referendum, may fatally have undermined the Union.

The referendum result was far from an expression of the settled will of the Scottish people. Nor was it a celebration of an invigorated Union. There was very little attempt by Better Together to offer a positive vision of a new progressive partnership between Scotland and England. It was a grudging No vote bought by threats and negativity. The campaign turned into a desperate last minute scramble. What looked at the start like a comfortable ride to victory for the Unionist coalition turned into a near-death experience for the British state.

CHAPTER TWO

The Devil You Know – The Pound and Disunion

On Tuesday 5th August 2014, as Alex Salmond walked onto the stage of Glasgow's Royal Conservatoire for his crucial televised debate with his Unionist opponent Alistair Darling, he knew that this could be the most important hour of his life. He had come a long way. Since he first became leader of the Scottish National Party in 1990, Salmond had dragged the SNP from obscurity to being the governing party of Scotland. He had played a key role in restoring the Scottish parliament after three hundred years in 1999; became First Minister in 2007; and went on to win an historic landslide victory in Holyrood in 2011 doing what no commentator thought possible – winning an absolute majority in a parliament elected using proportional representation. With the independence referendum now only weeks away, Salmond was in sight of the ultimate goal: bringing to an end one of the most successful political unions in history, which had once commanded an empire spanning a quarter of the planet. Yet it could all go wrong in the next sixty minutes. It very nearly did.

The build-up to the first gladiatorial encounter had been very positive for Salmond. Too positive. Commentators speculated that Alistair Darling would be ritually slaughtered by the foremost political debater of his generation. The First Minister was reported in *The Herald* as saying that Darling had the "heebie jeebies" about facing him in debate. Better Together carefully downplayed the chances of their own candidate. They were quoted in the *Daily Telegraph* as saying that Salmond would have to leave "Alistair lying on the floor in the foetal position crying" before it would have any impact on their lead in the opinion polls.[6] The twitterati were busy taking odds on how long it would take before Darling would be counted out.

I'd argued in my *Sunday Herald* column that this triumphalism was premature and struck the wrong note. For a start, the Yes Campaign was supposed to be above this kind of crude adversarial political banter. And while Alistair Darling had a reputation as a grey man he was no fool. Having been Labour's Chancellor of the Exchequer at the time of the banking crash in 2008, he had handled the near collapse of the UK financial system without panicking, curling into the foetal position, or crying on the floor. He was certainly no pushover and was on top of the numbers as far as the economy was concerned. He also loathed Alex Salmond with deep personal bitterness of the kind that only exists between leaders of Scotland's two tribes – Labour and the Scottish National Party.

I had been invited to be part of what STV had rather grandly titled the "spin room", which was really just the cafe area of the Royal Conservatoire, Glasgow's busiest performing arts venue. Journalists and representatives of the campaigns were supposed to watch the event on large screen TVs and then be interviewed by a roving STV presenter, John MacKay, for reaction. I was a little frustrated at not being allowed to see the debate in the flesh but there was nothing for it. At least we would be seeing the event as the vast majority of Scottish viewers would: on the box. As the crowds gathered, and the excitement mounted, the temperature rose fast, turning the spin room into a steam room.

The Yes campaign, who had commandeered the table directly in front of the main screen, were enjoying themselves hugely, looking around, taking selfies on their iPhones and iPads, and generally owning the room. The campaign leader Blair Jenkins held court with the former Bollywood actress, lawyer and SNP candidate Tasmina Ahmed-Sheikh, the pop singer turned cultural commentator Pat Kane, and the vivacious businesswoman Michelle Thomson of Business for Scotland. The seating plan was a resumé of Yes Scotland's inclusive gender-balanced and politician-free pitch to Scottish voters. Behind them sat a rather sober No table presided over by Glasgow University's Professor Adam Tomkins, and a selection of rather solemn-looking Labour women. They didn't look as if they were expecting a comfortable evening, having largely believed the inverted hype about their candidate's chances.

The debate was presided over by the robust figure of Bernard Ponsonby, the latest in a long line of STV political interviewers who bark their questions as if they are school-masters scolding primary children. In a puzzling lapse of judgement by ITV the event was not transmitted in England. Since this was the most important constitutional issue facing the UK at least since it joined the EEC, and arguably since 1707, many wondered just how significant a political event had to be to move the London programme controllers. STV gamely put the event on their digital player, which promptly crashed, meaning that it was impossible even to watch the event on the internet. Perhaps, for Alex Salmond, that was a good thing.

The candidates were permitted an opening statement. Salmond said that for half his adult life Scotland had been "governed by parties that Scots didn't vote for" and received in exchange objectionable policies from the poll tax to the bedroom tax. Scots, he said, should be "doing it for themselves". Darling stressed the need for unity. He said that "prosperity was better than borders" clearly marking out the economy, rather than democratic representation, as the terrain of battle. There were then some preliminary questions from the presenter that covered old ground and seemed to be dampening down the excitement in the packed auditorium. But the event came alive when the two politicians were let loose on each other. It was the worst twelve minutes of Alex Salmond's political career.

Darling had only one argument. Indeed, the entire Unionist case in the referendum rested on one simple proposition: Scotland would not have a currency union with the rest of the UK (rUK) after independence. "What's your Plan B, Alex, when you don't get the pound?", asked the former chancellor. Salmond responded that the pound was also "our pound", meaning Scotland's, and not "George Osborne's pound or your pound" and Scotland will keep it because "it is logical and desirable to have a common currency". The last sentence was a direct quote from an interview Alistair Darling had given to BBC's Newsnight the previous year. However, Darling was ready for this and pointed out that in the rest of the interview he'd said that it would never happen. "A currency union is stupidity on stilts. It only works if you have a political union," he said to cheers from the audience. "The flag is the saltire, the capital will still be Edinburgh. But you can't tell us what currency we will have."

Now, Alex Salmond has been rebutting questions like this at First Minster's questions almost weekly for seven long years. But suddenly he looked as if he was taken aback by the vehemence of the interrogation. He tried his trademark shrug of the shoulders and his half-smile of derision. But it wasn't working. He tried to rise above the finger pointing and be statesmanlike, not entering into the argy-bargy, but somehow this came across as evasion, even complacency. He tried to argue that a currency union would be "best for Scotland and best for the rest of the United

Kingdom". But Darling just talked over him. Salmond referred to an anonymous UK minister who had told *The Guardian* that "of course there would be a currency union" but Darling batted it aside as irrelevant. He jabbed his finger at Salmond and asked again and again, "what will the currency be of an independent Scotland. You can't say. You don't know. This is a disgrace". Salmond then tried to belittle Darling by suggesting he was trying to behave like Jeremy Paxman interviewing Michael Howard. But Darling raised another cheer as he bit back: "You're more like Michael Howard than Jeremy Paxman, First Minister". Howard had famously failed to answer a question on prisons after the *Newsnight* presenter had put it twelve times; Darling nearly equalled the record. Sweat appeared on the First Minister's lip, which could have been down to the overheated venue, or from nervousness. Either way, it looked bad.

But the worst was yet to come. When it came to Salmond's turn to challenge Alistair Darling, the FM began to look like an over-the-hill boxer who had gone back into the ring once too often. He asked the former Chancellor if he agreed with the Labour front-bencher Andy Burnham that after independence motorists would have to drive on the other side of the road. "Oh c'mon. He said it as a joke," said Darling, "you do know what a joke is, Alex?" This was true: it was *The Guardian*'s April Fool. Salmond then asked Darling if he agreed with Philip Hammond that "an independent Scotland would be more vulnerable to alien attack". Darling rightly dismissed this as time-wasting nonsense and said he'd rather talk about pensions and mortgages.

I learned afterwards that Salmond had personally chosen this line of questioning and had rehearsed until he was word perfect. They must have all had a great laugh at the time sending up independence scares. Unfortunately, no one in Salmond's prep team seemed to ask what the viewers would think of it. The Project Fear gibes were neither funny nor cutting, and it seemed demeaning for Scotland's First Minister to be wasting time on such trivia. Salmond had already missed one opportunity to shake Darling down after Ponsonby had asked him what extra powers the Scottish Parliament might acquire if Scotland voted No. The former Chancellor didn't seem to have an answer – which was potentially very damaging. But Salmond failed to press the advantage. Also, Darling squirmed when asked by Salmond whether he agreed with David Cameron that Scotland could be "a successful independent country". The chair of Better Together simply could not utter the words; it was a revealing moment. But by then the debate had already been lost by Salmond. The camera descended on the spin room for reaction, and of course it had to come to me first. "It wasn't Alex Salmond's best night", was the best I could do.

The debate had largely been what we in the trade call a "stairheid rammy", meaning a content-free dialogue of the deaf conducted at volume eleven. It wasn't a great start to the formal campaign. However, Darling had clearly won, and the ICM snap poll gave it to him by 56% to 44%, which was actually rather flattering to the First Minister. Darling's approach had not been pretty, but his barracking on the currency prevented Salmond from articulating his vision of a wealthy, healthy, egalitarian Scotland taking charge of its own destiny. The currency question could not be ignored.

By the next morning, Team Salmond was heavily into damage limitation. The First Minister arrived at the Business for Scotland conference in Edinburgh's Dynamic Earth armed with further analysis from the previous night's polling figures. Apparently this showed that his performance had been a modest hit with the voters, if not the journalists, which was a courageous interpretation. He said that Yes support had risen 2% in the two hours he was being pummelled by Darling's fickle finger of hate. ICM ended the night with the score on a binary basis at Yes 47% and No 53%. This was, Salmond boasted, the highest support for independence since the 2011 election. No one believed a word of it – not even the nationalist business people gathered before him. But in fact, this poll, at Salmond's darkest hour, was perhaps the first sign that the Yes campaign was actually making an impact, if not in the media, then certainly in the country. Only days before, the No campaign had had a 22 point lead – which was one reason Darling was so buoyant. Better Together was coasting to victory. Only it wasn't.

ST VALENTINE'S DAY SURPRISE

On the evidence of the first TV debate the Unionist strategy seemed to be going to plan. Better Together had elected to turn the referendum into what was essentially a single issue campaign based on the future of Scotland's currency. The policy was unveiled by the Chancellor George Osborne on the eve of St Valentine's Day 2014. Osborne came to Scotland on a day trip to deliver, before an invited audience, a blunt threat to the Scots: "The pound isn't an asset to be divided up between two countries after a break up like a CD collection", he said. "If Scotland walks away from the UK, it walks away from the UK Pound". The Tory Chancellor then walked away himself, refusing to give any television interviews, visibly angering STV's political editor, Bernard Ponsonby, who pursued him all the way to his waiting people carrier, firing questions. It was the key moment of the entire campaign. The previous two years since the signing of the Edinburgh Agreement, in which Alex Salmond and David Cameron had agreed on the referendum ground rules, had all been shadow boxing. This was the killer blow.

The attraction of the pound exclusion strategy was its simplicity. It focussed attention on the area where Alex Salmond and the Yes Campaign were weakest: the economy. Opinion surveys and focus groups had indicated that Scottish voters, while many found the idea of independence appealing, believed that it carried unquantifiable risks. Scots did not feel oppressed in any way by England, and they did not need national liberation from a Union in which Scottish identity was given free expression. Consequently, the nationalists had to base their campaign, not on "freedom" but on an argument that Scotland could be a more prosperous and fairer country if it took charge of its own affairs. Not an easy task. At the very least, canny middle-class voters would have to be persuaded that they would not lose out under independence. The Chancellor, by making clear in advance that Scotland would not be allowed to use the pound after independence, magnified the risks and allowed a sympathetic press to portray Alex Salmond as a reckless gambler with no credible economic plan, who was willing to play politics with peoples' livelihoods.

What George Osborne was saying, in effect, was that the rUK would not lift a finger to assist an independent Scotland to get on its financial feet. It would, perhaps literally, erect monetary border posts forcing Scots to change currency when they visited their relatives in England. Bereft of sterling, an independent Scotland would have to set up its own currency, or issue a "shadow pound", carrying the risk that borrowing costs would be high at least in the early years of independence. Moreover, by rejecting monetary union, the UK forced many Scottish businesses to deliver guidance to their shareholders that their performance could be damaged by "exchange rate uncertainty and currency risk". Many banks would have to consider relocating their registered headquarters to London, not because they wanted to but because that was the only way to guarantee that they remained under the protection of the Bank of England as "lender of last resort".

Alistair Darling, the chair of Better Together, was the architect of this entire approach. Having been Chancellor at the time of the financial crash, he knew only too well how important the Bank of England had been in rescuing Scotland's delinquent banks, RBS and HBOS, from the consequences of their own folly. He also hoped to remind Scots of the fate of small independent countries like Iceland and Ireland – formerly part of what Alex Salmond had called the "arc of prosperity" – which had suffered catastrophic banking failures leading to inflation, public spending cuts, unemployment, and real estate crashes. Why take the risk? Scotland is better together with the strength of the UK economy to fall back on.

Monetary exclusion was a tough-minded policy, even a brutal one; almost a threat of economic isolation. The *Sunday Herald*, the only paper to support Yes, said Osborne was playing "Dirty Harry politics" holding a gun to Scotland's head and saying: "Do you feel lucky, punk"? It certainly seemed to be like part of a "good cop/bad cop" routine by the UK government. David Cameron's approach had been much more emollient, saying in early February in an address at the London Olympic stadium that he would be "heartbroken" if Scotland left the Union and making emotional appeals, echoing celebrities like David Bowie, to "please stay". But the Declaration on the Pound as it became known was the pivotal moment in the entire referendum, and the impact was immediate. Standard Life, one of Scotland's biggest finance houses, announced that it was making contingency plans to move at least some of its activities to London. Speculation mounted that RBS would have to relocate its registered HQ. A succession of big businesses, Agrekko, BP, Sainsbury's, delivered warnings that currency uncertainty was likely to cause job losses, supermarket price rises, and cancelled investment plans.

The UK press, which had been speculating about this announcement for weeks, went into full panic mode. *The Times* said following Osborne's speech, "Chancellor Crushes All Hope of Using the Pound". "Salmond Has Nowhere Left to Hide" said the front page of the *Daily Express*. The *Daily Mail* had "Salmond Ducks Out – With His Currency Plan Blown to Pieces". By the weekend, the newspapers were filled with reports from the British Retail Consortium suggesting that famous brand name firms like Tesco, John Lewis, Marks and Spencer might have to "redomicile" because of uncertainty over the pound. Of course, the idea that these firms would actually leave Scotland, a valuable market, was absurd, but the headlines conveyed the impression of a positive stampede of big businesses heading for the exit door. Not for nothing was the Chancellor's strategy called "shock and awe", or "Shock and Naw", as some wags put it on the internet.

Alex Salmond said, alternately, that the Chancellor was "bluffing" and "bullying" and the Yes campaign never quite decided which they thought it was. A currency union had seemed like a sensible proposal, at least to SNP ministers. In some respects it was, and there were historical precedents. In the 1950s and 60s, when African countries achieved independence from the British Empire and sought to set up their own central banks and currencies, the UK government tried to keep them all together in a sterling zone. Indeed, the Bank of England sent officials to countries like Ghana and Nigeria urging them to keep the pound as their currency.[i][7]

The Scottish Government, somewhat naively, thought that the UK might threaten to exclude Scotland from the pound, but would never actually do it. Would the UK treat Scotland worse than a former colony? Anyway, it seemed manifestly to be in the economic interest of the rUK to keep trade free of exchange risk and transaction costs with one of its biggest trading partners. The Vice-Chancellor of Glasgow University, Professor Anton Muscatelli – a prominent non-nationalist economist – said in the *Financial Times*

---

i The Commonwealth of former British colonies and dependencies was always meant to be a single currency zone using the pound. And though the sterling area disintegrated in the 1960s, this was as John Chown put it, "a genuine monetary union" (John F. Chown, *The History of Monetary Unions*, p. 109). It was an important reason why the UK resisted joining the EEC. As David Gowland explains: "The sterling zone operated as a monetary union in which sterling was the major reserve currency and Britain acted as the central banker supervising the common pool of the area's exchange reserves" (*Britain and European Integration 1945-1998: A Documentary History* edited by David Gowland and Arthur Turner, p. 62). Could this not have been a model for Scotland after independence?

that it would be "tantamount to economic vandalism" for the UK to refuse a currency union.[8] Yet here was the Chancellor of the Exchequer ruling it out without negotiation, qualification or possibility of review. And he was supported that very day by the Liberal Democrat Treasury Secretary, Danny Alexander and by Ed Balls, the Labour Shadow Chancellor. Indeed, the Labour leader, Ed Miliband, even promised to put rejection of a currency union with Scotland in the next UK Labour general election manifesto.

The UK opposition leaders said that the eurozone crisis had shown that monetary unions don't work without political union, which was a sweeping assessment. Certainly, monetary unions between unbalanced economies like Germany and Greece, which have very different rates of labour productivity, had difficulties. But as the Governor of the Bank of England had said on 29th January 2014, in many ways Scotland and England were already an "optimal currency zone" in terms of GDP, trading links and labour productivity. Many UK economists must have privately wondered about the wisdom of the Unionist policy. Was it sensible to close off monetary options at this stage? Should there not be scope at least for negotiation? The anonymous government minister Alex Salmond referred to had told *The Guardian* in April 2014 that "of course there would be a currency union".[9] But the economists mostly kept their own council, and the official line was "Scotland – you're on your own".

The Scottish Government had already lined up its own team of top economists, including Nobel-laureates like Professor Joseph Stiglitz and Professor James Mirlees, in its Fiscal Commission to argue the contrary. They had said that currency union was the best outcome for the rUK as well as Scotland – at least in the short term – because it ensured continuity of trade and would reassure financial markets. But what they didn't take into account was that the authors of the Better Together strategy didn't really want calm financial markets; they wanted the threat of a flight of funds from Scotland. It was something they very nearly achieved too, though what they perhaps didn't expect was that funds flowed equally from the rest of the UK. The referendum campaign saw the largest capital flight from Britain since the collapse of Lehman Brothers in 2008. This was financial scorched earth.[10]

PLAN B

The Scottish Government was clearly taken aback by the currency lock out and really had no answer to it. Alex Salmond just kept saying, truthfully but lamely, "there is no plan B", and that he believed the rUK would come round to the idea of a currency union. In fact, the Fiscal Commission had looked at several Plan Bs including so-called "sterlingisation" under which Scotland would issue its own pound pegged to sterling. But the Fiscal Commissioners reasoned that none of the alternatives to currency union would ensure stability and continuity. They also believed that the Chancellor was bluffing.

Some prominent figures in the Yes campaign had argued for Scotland to have a separate currency on principle, including Alex Salmond's former SNP mentor, Jim Sillars, and the leader of the Scottish Green Party, Patrick Harvie. They argued that Scotland could not call itself independent if it continued to rely on the Bank of England to set interest rates and limit economic freedom. The Governor of the Bank of England, Mark Carney, had said that a currency union was "incompatible with sovereignty"and suggested that not only interest rates, but public spending and borrowing might have to be controlled in Scotland by UK institutions to avoid sovereign debt crises. But the matter had never been thrashed out between the various groups supporting independence.[11] And as these key figures departed from the Salmond line of "currency union, nothing less", the press were able to say that the Yes campaign was at sixes and sevens over the pound. It was undoubtedly a mess. A number of key figures in the Yes Scotland campaign told me that they believed the dogmatic line on the currency had come directly from Alex Salmond. They felt the rejection of Plan B had undermined the independence campaign and failed to address the reality that Westminster had simply said no to currency union.

Belatedly, the Scottish Government came up with a response of a kind, which was to argue that, if Scotland was not permitted to use the pound, one of the key assets of the Union, then it could not be expected to pay its share of the interest on the UK national debt – which amounted to some £5 billion a year. This was certainly an option. It's not entirely clear how the markets would have reacted to it, however. Alistair Darling and most of the UK press said that Salmond was threatening to "default on Scotland's debt".

This led to speculation that Scotland's cost of borrowing would rocket after independence: ratings agencies like Standard and Poor suggested that they very well might in the short term, even though Scotland's debt would be "investment grade". In reply to the Scottish Government's Finance Secretary, John Swinney, Mark Carney said that if Scotland tried this, it would have to accumulate currency reserves up to 100% of GDP, or over £100 billion.[12]

If the Scottish Government had thought that the governor would maintain a detached Olympian stance on the referendum, then that was another miscalculation. Carney became a key player and in the final weeks would infuriate the Scottish Government further by suggesting that the bank would expect to have power, not just over interest rates and borrowing, but also taxation in an independent Scotland. In remarks to the TUC ten days before the referendum poll, he said that currency union required "some form of fiscal arrangement. You need tax, revenues and spending flowing across those borders to help equalise, to an extent, some of the inevitable differences [across the union]".[13] John Swinney insisted that this was not the case. France, Finland and Austria share a currency but have 100% control of their own tax. But this dispute just gave the press another chance to rubbish the Scottish Government's independence policy.

THE ECONOMIC EQUIVALENT OF WAR

Those in the Yes campaign who thought the UK government, the Westminster parties, and the Bank of England would play cricket with the Scottish Government were forced to think again. This looked very much like the economic equivalent of war, said one SNP insider. Indeed, a source in the coalition was reported in *The Herald* as describing the pound policy as the "Dambusters strategy"[14] – first detonate the bomb of the pound and watch the businesses flow out of Scotland like water from the Moehne dam. However, the mistake the Treasury made was to forget that aerial bombardment, like the London Blitz, tends to unite the people who are being bombed and encourage resistance. And that is actually what happened in Scotland.

There was initial shock, certainly among the Scottish voters, when the Chief Secretary to the Treasury, Danny Alexander, said that in an independent Scotland people could expect to be up to £5,000 a year worse off. But they weren't perhaps as worried as they should have been. Indeed, there was an immediate groundswell of resentment expressed in social media that bankers should not be dictating the constitutional future of Scotland. As the *Sunday Herald* pointed out, firms like Royal Bank of Scotland were not exactly top of the Scottish voters' popularity charts. Indeed the former CEO of RBS "Sir" Fred Goodwin had become a virtual public enemy in Scotland when he refused to hand back any of his ill-gotten gains after the taxpayer bail out of his bank. Standard Life, for its part, had made very similar negative noises about devolution before the last Scottish referendum in 1997. The image being presented to Scots was that Better Together –and by association, the Union itself – was essentially a coalition of bankers, big business and Westminster Tory politicians. This was not the way to win the hearts and minds of Scotland, an essentially social democratic country in which "Tory" is still a four-letter word.

The UK and Scottish press seemed largely oblivious to this groundswell of resistance among their readers and continued to feature shock headlines throughout the months following the Declaration on the Pound. Pension providers reported that pensions funds could be hit. Scottish accountants warned of financial risk and instability. The Institute for Fiscal Studies calculated that an independent Scotland would likely have a deficit in the early years of around 6% of GDP, which would require tax increases or spending cuts. This was a highly damaging report from a respected source. However, it was based on pessimistic projections of the likely future revenue from North Sea oil, which the Scottish Government refuted, and also on a forecast of Scotland's ageing population that Alex Salmond said was the result of UK immigration policies and a lack of jobs. The Union hit back with a claim by the billionaire oil tycoon Sir Ian Wood that North Sea oil was running out fast. The Yes campaign pointed out that Sir Ian had himself issued a report the previous February arguing that there was "up to 24bn barrels" left, worth "£200bn for the economy".

But the dominance of the currency issue made it very difficult for the Scottish Government to get its message across. Set out in its voluminous White Paper *Scotland's Future* in November 2013, it asserted that, with independence, Scotland could promote growth policies and make better use of natural resources like oil and green energy. There was undoubtedly an economic case to be made here. Scotland's GDP is one of the highest in the world, 14th according to the OECD. Scotland has five world class universities, most of Europe's oil reserves, much of Europe's renewable energy, a financial services sector employing 100,000 people, food and drink exports worth £8bn a year, a world class tourist industry worth £4bn, strengths in life sciences and advanced engineering. On this prospectus, Scotland could certainly become one of those small dynamic Northern European countries which had been making such a success of globalisation. As a report from Credit Suisse, 'The Success of Small Nations', had observed in July, the emergence of these prosperous small counties has been "one of the great mega-trends of the 21st Century". In terms of wealth, quality of life and social solidarity, they easily out pace the older, larger countries.[15]

Even David Cameron had agreed that Scotland could be a successful independent country, all things being equal. However, the point was that all things were not equal. By denying Scotland use of the pound, the UK Chancellor prevented Scotland's positive case for independence getting to first base. What was the point of having all this potential, if an independent Scotland was going to become a financial basket case on day one? Scotland would be forced to incur hugely increased borrowing costs because of currency instability. Growth policies? Most of Scotland's exports go to England, but England was saying that they would not only impose transfer costs on those exports, but also encourage many of Scotland's businesses to move south. Financial services? Without the pound? A joke – and anyway, weren't the banks and insurance companies all leaving? The Declaration on the Pound was intended to wreck the Scottish Government's plans, and it did. However, what no one realised, on either side, was that it was also about to come close to wrecking the Better Together campaign.

THE SILENT CURRENCY BACKLASH

The signs were there within weeks of the Chancellor's speech, though few took them seriously. Opinion polls reported that support for independence had increased marginally in the wake of the pound declaration. But more importantly for Better Together, they indicated that most Scots didn't believe the

Chancellor was serious.[16] In fact, the credibility problem got worse for Better Together as the referendum approached and by August, when the official campaign began, even a majority of No voters said they simply did not believe the Chancellor and the Leader of the Opposition on the pound. In the Scottish Social Attitudes Survey, which tends not to be favourable to independence, the vast majority of voters agreed with Alex Salmond that there should be a monetary union, and most thought there would be. The UK's leading polling analyst, Professor John Curtice, gave this assessment of the overall polling evidence in his blog, *What Scotland Thinks* on 2nd September 2014: "67% of Scottish voters believe that an independent Scotland would carry on using the pound. Amongst Yes voters that last figure stands at no less than 87%, including 67% who think there would still be a monetary union, but even just over half of No voters, 54%, reckon Scotland would keep the pound. In short the No side's claim that an independent Scotland would not be able to keep the pound is still widely disbelieved".[17] This was an extraordinary development, which even some in the Yes campaign found hard to credit. The Scottish Government's entire economic policy lay in ruins, and yet the Scots were saying: well, actually, we prefer the ruins.

Throughout April and May, there were persistent rumours on the internet that opinion polls conducted by the UK government had shown a dramatic increase in Yes support and that the No campaign was keeping them secret. In fact, the private polls weren't saying anything very different from the published ones. It's just that no one in the UK government could quite believe them. The Yes campaign was way behind overall, and yet Scots appeared to be rejecting the key policy on which the entire Unionist case rested. Better Together persuaded themselves that this didn't really matter, and that perhaps some Scots were just making clear they didn't like to dance to London's tune. On the bigger question of the Union the Scots were mostly still saying, politely, that they really didn't want to leave the UK, which was – well – family. And that was true; they didn't. But the pound thing – well, that was another matter entirely.

The first Unionist to realise the enormity of what was happening was probably the former Prime Minister Gordon Brown. He had been largely out of politics since his departure from Number Ten under a dark cloud in June 2010. But he was as keen an observer of politics in Scotland as ever and Brown realised by May that the monetary bluff had been called. On June 2nd, he went public and infuriated Better Together by echoing Alex Salmond's claim that Scotland was being "bullied". In an interview with the *Daily Record* the former Labour PM said "The way the currency argument was put by the Government made the issue Scotland versus Britain... But if the only propaganda that comes from the Conservatives is, 'Britain says No', it's bound to have a reaction in Scotland. It is bound to make people feel that people are talking down to us or are not taking us seriously or are trying to bully us." Brown became more and more disillusioned with the negativity of the Better Together campaign, and in the end, he launched his own.

The failure of the pound strategy left Better Together in an awkward place. Having believed that the negative case would win, they hadn't developed a coherent or positive one. This should have been done in May when the Scottish opposition parties finally put together their offerings of more powers for Holyrood. But unfortunately, they all said different things. No common platform emerged until three days before polling day when, under pressure from Gordon Brown's Midlothian campaign, the three UK party leaders signed the solemn and binding "vow" on more powers.

While the Chancellor's currency bluff was being called, the network of community groups created by Blair Jenkins' Yes Scotland campaign had begun to work a grassroots political conversion of biblical proportions. I first received notice of this in early August when contacts in the Scottish Government started becoming inexplicably bullish about the possibility of a Yes victory. Yet, at the time, Better Together's lead seemed as solid as ever. But what was happening was that on the ground the Yes campaign was discovering that Scottish voters were turning to independence, not just in their tens of thousands but possibly in their hundreds of thousands. Support for independence was spreading like wildfire through the council estates of Scotland, particularly in Labour areas like Dundee, North Lanarkshire, and Glasgow. However, the headline opinion polls didn't start seriously to move until after Alex Salmond's second, final encounter with Alistair Darling on 25th August, which was a very different affair from their first. In only three weeks it appeared the world had changed.

ROUND TWO

The second round of the Great Debate took place amid the blood-red sandstone of Glasgow's Kelvingrove Museum, an ornate building erected in the Spanish Baroque style in 1888 which houses the city art collection. Both sides favoured cultural venues over political ones in the hope of elevating the debate. The BBC had commandeered the vast museum and I, along with the rest of the UK and the international press contingent, had to watch on video screens in the basement. But this time the world was watching. And from the moment Salmond walked onto the stage it was clear that this was not going to be a repeat of his pasting in round one.

The First Minister still didn't have any coherent answer when asked about the currency of an independent Scotland, but somehow it didn't seem to matter this time. He said confusingly that he had "offered three plan B's for the price of one". He then said "of course Scotland could use the pound", claiming to have quoted Alistair Darling though the words were taken out of context. Salmond then asked the Better Together chairman if he would accept "the mandate of the Scottish people" and campaign for a currency union if there was a Yes in the referendum. This begged the question of whether there would be a "mandate" from the people of England for currency union, since most polls showed English voters were opposed to one. But the ploy was to place Darling on the "other side" of the debate on Scotland, with the Tories and the banks instead of "the people". And it seemed to work.

Salmond also invoked in this debate the privatisation of the NHS, which had unexpectedly turned out to be a key issue in the "ground war" even though health is devolved. Would privatisation of health be a price worth paying for the Union, he asked? Would 100,000 children be forced into poverty? Trident, the bedroom tax? It was all pretty low politics, but it forced Darling to appear to defend UK Coalition policies. "You're in bed with the Tories", cried Salmond in triumph. The ICM/*Guardian* snap poll this time gave the victory to Salmond by 71% to 29%. Even the *Daily Mail* was impressed: "Salmond Bounces Back; SNP Leader Crushes Weak Darling in Second TV Debate".

Of course, these televised debates were not where the real campaign was being fought. That was out in the constituencies where grassroots organisations like Radical Independence were encouraging people to register to vote in unprecedented numbers. The TV debates were just part of the theatre of the campaign: theatre is important so long as it is all right on the night. The reason Salmond found the second debate so much easier was the knowledge that support for Yes was rising. The opposition to the Coalition's policy on the pound had been building up for months; but it was only in August that Scots concluded that this meant Scotland should leave the UK. The second TV debate seemed to be the cue for Scots to start translating their resentment into active support for independence.

Almost from the moment Alex Salmond walked off the Kelvingrove stage, Yes support started to grow fast until, on September 6th 2014, YouGov reported that, for the first time, Yes had taken the lead in a reputable opinion poll. Better Together's huge lead had evaporated in a month, confounding pollsters and leaving the Yes campaign confident of victory. The final ten days of the campaign were more hectic than anything anyone could remember. Ed Miliband led over a hundred Labour MPs across the border for a last minute push. UK journalists descended on Scotland, tripping over their prejudices and misconceptions. David Cameron, in a speech to employees of Scottish Widows in Edinburgh, pleaded with Scots not to vote for independence "just to give the effing Tories a kicking". The Unionist parties started offering Scots more powers for Holyrood.

As we know, Scots pulled back from the brink. A combination of Gordon Brown's advocacy – his Glasgow speech on the eve of poll was certainly a formidable one – the Vow on more powers, and the fears of currency isolation prevailed. Older and middle-class voters undoubtedly responded to the warnings over financial insecurity. And many in the independence movement, such as Robin McAlpine of Common Weal, have said since the referendum that there had been there had been a failure on the part of the Yes Scotland campaign to mobilise an effective economic counterargument. The UK had delivered a threat of monetary exclusion, and the Scottish Government had not responded in kind. Too often it relied on faith, hope and assertions that

Scotland was "a wealthy country". Next time, if there is a next time, supporters of independence will have to find a way to calm the fears of mortgage owners, pensioners and people with shares in Scottish and UK companies. That is never easy for a radical movement that put social justice and equality at the top of its agenda. But the hard arithmetic of independence is that it cannot be won if the middle-classes, or at least a significant portion of them, are not on board. Some of the far left groups in the fringe of the independence movement might find this particularly difficult. But who exactly were they?

One of the most vocal groups was the Radical Independence Campaign. Born at a conference in Edinburgh in 2012, it brought together elements of the old far left with the Greens and large numbers of disillusioned Labour supporters. It had grown fast, having 1000 supporters at its second plenary in Glasgow in November 2013, and then had to book a 3000 capacity venue for its 2014 conference. The mass canvasses organised by RIC played a significant role in many council estates in traditionally Labour areas like Glasgow and North Lanarkshire. RIC is also the group that forced the UKIP leader Nigel Farage to take refuge in a pub in Edinburgh's Royal Mile during his visit to Scotland in 2013, not because he was English, but because of UKIP policies on immigration and welfare. The Radical Independence Campaign was co-founded by Jonathon Shafi, a member of the International Socialist Group, which broke from the Socialist Workers Party because of the latter's hostility to nationalism, though the SWP puzzlingly went on to became an active supporter of the Yes campaign. ISG has a number of prominent young activists, including the flame headed Cat Boyd, a trade union youth organiser with Public and Commerical Services Union, who has become a celebrity on the indy left.

The biggest far left group in RIC is the Scottish Socialist Party, led by the former MSP Colin Fox, who is also on the organising committee of the official Yes Scotland campaign. The SSP was the most successful far left group in Scotland having once had no fewer than six MSPs in the Scottish Parliament. It is directly descended from Militant Tendency and its former star was Tommy Sheridan, the firebrand leader of the anti-poll tax campaign in the late 1980s, though it fell out with him over Sheridan's defamation action against the *News of the World* in 2006. That split led to the loss of all the SSP MSPs in the 2007 Scottish parliamentary elections.

There is more than a hint of Monty Python's Popular Front of Judea about the fragments of the indy left and their interconnections. Ironically, in 2014, the SSP found itself fighting the cause in the independence campaign alongside its former leader, Tommy Sheridan, now of Solidarity Scotland. The SSP prevented Sheridan from actually joining the Radical Independence Campaign (old enmities die hard) but the former anti-poll tax campaigner conducted his own barn-storming tour of central Scotland, addressing 25,000 people during the campaign as a kind of Trotskyite Gordon Brown. His campaign, Hope over Fear, managed to attract 7,000 people to a demonstration in Glasgow's George Square on 12 October 2014.[18] Just to add to the confusion, the Socialist Workers Party backed Sheridan's Solidarity campaign, though they have now broken from him over his call for the left to vote SNP at the next general election.

This factionalism is of course typical of the far left. However, by working with the Green Party in the Radical Independence Campaign they managed to overcome their differences, at least for the duration of the referendum. The Green Party itself brought to RIC large numbers of people from environmental groups in Scotland like Friends of the Earth, People and Planet, Greenpeace, and many local green organisations like the Fife Diet (more on this later). Also linked is the Scottish peace movement, centred around the Scottish CND, led by John Ainslie.

The other significant group to emerge from the referendum campaign which had no immediate connection with the SNP was the Common Weal, a think tank – or as it prefers to be known a "do-tank" – led by Robin McAlpine, a former public affairs officer for Scottish universities. Common Weal emerged from the Jimmy Reid Foundation, a body set up to celebrate the life of the late Communist leader of the Upper Clyde Shipbuilders work-in in 1971. Reid latterly became a supporter of independence and the foundation that bears his name explores that legacy. The Common Weal departed from the Jimmy Reid Foundation after an acrimonious split last year and accusations of "ego tripping" by the hyperactive McAlpine, which he dismisses.

Unlike the far left, the Common Weal does not argue for state ownership as such – though it isn't against it for natural monopolies like rail – and has instead tried to develop a model of what might be called Nordic stakeholder capitalism. It is a vision of a dynamic, industrial market economy based on high incomes, low wealth differentials, worker participation and high social protections. It has been accused of economic naiveté, partly because it doesn't use an off-the-peg Marxist analysis to criticise capitalism, but relies on localism and cooperative ideas derived from the environmental movement. But what it lacks in sophistication it makes up for in sheer energy. The SNP has largely accepted a version of the Common Weal programme and it has a number of small business supporters in Business for Scotland.

Business for Scotland, usually represented by its youthful Managing Director, Michell Thomson, sought to make what might be called the capitalist case for independence. But neoliberal it isn't. Unlike most business organisations BforS opposes austerity, supports public spending and even seems to advocate increased personal taxation. It doesn't even seem to be particularly keen on the SNP's policy of cutting corporation tax by 3p below the UK rate. Business for Scotland claims around two thousand members, and it has been criticised for only representing small and intermediate, rather than big UK firms, though it did claim in its ranks the controversial Brian Souter, of Stagecoach fame, Sir George Matthewson, formerly of the Royal Bank, and Jim McColl of Clyde Blowers. Despite being an odds on to lose the referendum, Yes even attracted the support of the former head of William Hill book-makers, Ralph Topping. It may seem strange that all these people could be united behind the same banner as groups like the Scottish Socialists, Tommy Shereidan, and ISG, but such is the nature of nationalism that it can mobilise across class boundaries. Scottish businesses felt the threat of monetary isolation particularly acutely. If Better Together thought businesspeople would automatically back the Union out of fear of financial instability, they were wrong.

The pound exclusion changed the relationship between Scotland and England, if only because no one north of the border can be in any doubt now that the Union has ceased to be a partnership of equals, at least as far as currency is concerned. The eurozone crisis has raised questions about the viability of monetary unions without political union. Nevertheless, it appeared to many as if the UK was behaving like an old style, pre-Harold McMillan imperial power, trying to bully and threaten Scotland into sticking with the Union rather than offering it as a great common project. The rejection of currency union, out of hand and without possibility of negotiation, sent a disturbing message to many younger Scots: that the rUK was prepared, if necessary, to wreck the Scottish economy rather than let Scotland go. History may judge that, as a moral community, the Union died on 13th February 2014, and that it was George Osborne who wielded the knife.

CHAPTER THREE

The Pure, The Dead and The Brilliant – How Art became Politics

In early May 2014 I received a call from a photographer and PR consultant called Linda Graham. Over coffee she said she thought that it would be possible to do live television for the referendum and that she'd registered the domain name, Referendum TV. What did I think? Well, I thought it was, er, interesting. I'd worked as a BBC presenter for nearly twenty years and I'd seen a few attempts on the internet to emulate the established broadcasters and hadn't been impressed.

The slogan "don't bemoan the media, become the media" has a great ring to it, but in practice it usually means: become a very good reason to leave this kind of stuff to the BBC. To do a live television show, even a talk show, sounds relatively simple but is complex in ways that only people who've worked in TV can understand. It is not just technically demanding, but requires sound editorial discretion, knowledge of the law, and a large number of people with a clear idea of what they are trying to do. It also needs a shed load of money.

This venture had no money and no people, but somehow it happened and I'm still not entirely sure how. As was the case with so many creative activities during the referendum campaign, the people somehow emerged, from small independent media companies, universities and colleges, from various Yes supporting campaigns. No political party was involved in the making of these programmes and certainly not the Scottish National Party. Backed by a tiny sum from crowdsourcing and relying on unpaid volunteers, it got the show on the road.

Like many Yes activists, Linda Graham had a skill with information technology and was able to reduce a TV control room – which normally involves a vast desk with a vision mixer and banks of video monitors – to a couple of PCs. People came up with cameras – pretty much off the shelf – and various bits and pieces, the names for which I never actually learned. Alison Balharry used her expertise as a former BBC producer to put the content together. Lesley Riddoch, one of the best live broadcasters around who had been ejected from the BBC some years ago, essentially for not being boring, was the lead presenter along with Sarah Beattie Smith from the Green Party and yours truly.

The show came live from a Fringe Venue, the Hill Street Theatre, courtesy of Tomek Borkowy, a Polish actor who runs the production company Universal Arts and who had escaped from Poland in 1981 when it was still under martial law. There are nearly 100,000 Polish-born people living in Scotland and many were active in the Yes campaign, though Tomek was upset that many had been told by Better Together people that they would be sent home if Scotland became independent.

Referendum TV was webcast before a live audience daily at one 1pm throughout the 2014 Edinburgh Festival, after which we all parted company. And it really wasn't bad, despite my frequent gaffes which included getting my own name wrong a couple of times. The idea was not to replace the BBC but to do things in a different way, and to speak to the kind of people who were currently making history in real time across Scotland but were below the radar of the mainstream media. The show had a clear political centre of gravity but was not a piece of nationalist propaganda and gave space for intelligent Unionists like Simon Pia and Alex Massie. And while it had rough edges, it rapidly developed its own style.

Instead of the "drive-by" tradition of BBC television, the interviewees were allowed time to develop their arguments without constant interruptions from a "look-at-me" presenter. It was long-form interviewing and generated some real surprises, as when the fiercely Unionist Lord George Foulkes – a relentless opponent of the SNP – told a bemused Hill St audience that he supported a federal future for the UK, with a senate replacing the House of Lords and a state parliament for Scotland with extensive economic powers. There were contributions from journalists and writers like Neal Ascherson, and the former BBC Moscow correspondent Angus Roxburgh, who both had extensive knowledge of nationalist movements in central and eastern Europe. Referendum TV also became a showcase, inevitably, for big-name film, stage, and TV actors connected with the independence movement, like David Hayman whose 'Pitiless Storm' was running at the Edinburgh Festival. Then there was the ubiquitous Elaine C Smith who starred in a range of productions including Alan Bissett's satirical comedy 'The Pure, The Dead and the Brilliant', which looked at the independence campaign through the eyes of banshees, demons and creatures from Scottish folk mythology. The devil doesn't have all the best tunes after all.

Of course, these celebs get plenty of coverage on the conventional media. Referendum TV made a point of speaking to many individuals and small groups who were largely unknown before the referendum. People making films, opening political cafes, staging events, writing plays, making music, and generally enjoying themselves in their politics. It was a remarkable insight into the kind of creative energy unleashed by the independence campaign. I just remember a blur of enthusiastic faces including Helen Marnie from the group Ladytron, the graphic artist Stewart Bremner, cartoonist and author Greg Moodie, Zara Gladman aka Lady Alba, a keenly observed pro-indy parody of the pop singer, Lady Gaga. There were comedians like Phil Differ of 'MacBraveheart'; film-makers like Christopher Silver and Jack Foster who made the feature film *Scotland Yet*; also new media figures like Stephen Paton of 'Indyref Weekly Report' who was also one of the presentation team. There was also Chris Hill, former mountaineer, who took a 1950s Green Goddess army fire-engine, painted blue and called the Spirit of Independence, across Scotland staging events and debates. Mike Small, of the website Bella Caledonia, discussed the state of the media and his plans for replacing the BBC. There was a procession too of the various subdivisions of the Yes Campaign: Generation Yes, Women for Independence, Asians for Independence, Polish for Independence, English for Independence.

There was simply a hell of a lot of art going on everywhere. Many events were as much cultural as political, like the ImagiNation festival in Glasgow in September held in Govanhill Baths, organised by Gerry Hassan and Roanne Dods. This had music, films and readings as well as political discussions and was rounded up by songs from Billy Bragg. At the Glasgow Film Festival, work by the film-maker Rachel Maclean, exploring identity through kitsch and grotesque imagery, provided a vivid hyper-realist backdrop for an examination of the cultural impact of the independence campaign. These are things that remain in the mind long after the political arguments have moved on.

The playwright David Greig was one of the key figures in the non-aligned Yes campaign through his plays, countless speaking engagements, and shows like 'All Back To Bowies' at the Edinburgh Festival Fringe. This was a discursive send up of the singer David

Bowie's call at the Brit Awards in February for Scotland to stay in the Union. Greig is, of course, an established playwright and theatre director whose work has been performed in London and across the world, and he became a kind of cultural curator for the referendum as well as a campaigner. His Yes/No plays on Twitter – delivered 140 characters at a time – provided a witty and often moving commentary on Scotland's agonies of indecision over self-government. He is convinced that the cultural dimension of the referendum campaign was what made it unique. "It was more like the Summer of Love than a normal political campaign" he says, only half-joking. "It affected people so deeply because it wasn't exclusive. People were invited in and encouraged to contribute." Some of the cultural products, he admits, were of indifferent quality but the enthusiasm was the key.

Others took a very different view of the role of art in politics. The Director of the Edinburgh International Festival, Jonathan Mills, had said in 2013 that he didn't think the Edinburgh Festival was the place for works about independence. "Calls for the Festival to engage in an explicit or overt debate about independence are, I believe, a misunderstanding of the role of the Festival." Well, the artistic community had other ideas and while the official Festival tried to ignore the referendum, the Edinburgh Festival Fringe was overflowing with plays, music and debates. And really, if the arts aren't there to explore the great political and ideological issues of the day you wonder what they are there for. How can art possibly ignore identity, meaning and history? I suspect that, underlying Mills' reluctance to engage with the constitutional debate, was the perennial unease about nationalism, and the presumption that the Yes campaign, all evidence to the contrary, must in some way have been about the "dark side" of politics.

There was much suspicion also that many of the cultural initiatives that appeared during the referendum weren't truly spontaneous and had been set up by the SNP. The proliferation of Yes campaigns was in part a result of election finance rules which allowed organisations which supported independence to spend up to £150,000 so long as they were registered and did not co-ordinate their activities. It is true that the largest of them, National Collective, set up in 2011 by the graphic artist Ross Colquhoun, was registered as part of the campaign. But from the start it had a life of its own, was completely self-financing, and none of the creative figures involved were paid any money by anyone. The core group in the collective included the writer/map maker Andrew Redmond Barr, the poet and singer Karine Polwart, lecturer and "ethnomusicographer" Mairi McFadyen, and writer Miriam Bett. National Collective went on to mobilise 1,300 artists, writers and performers in support of the Yes campaign, mostly obscure, but many very well known, like the poet Alan Riach, writer AL Kennedy, and playwright Alan Bissett. National Collective made a point of targeting younger age groups and most of its readers/audience were between 16 and 34 years of age. But it didn't talk down to them, as any visit to the website will confirm. There are long-form essays on everything from philosophy to fiscal autonomy. The collective's essay on the referendum result was read by 200,000 and tweeted by 75,000. Its #YesBecause twitter campaign was seen by 3 million.

National Collective is a difficult organisation to define since it did everything, from producing a magazine to making videos, mounting theatrical productions, and staging music and comedy events. It provided a cultural resource-base for its network of local groups. A kind of "dial-a-poet" service. In the summer of 2014 the Collective raised £31,000 by crowdfunding and turned the referendum campaign into a rolling festival, or Yestival, full of colour, wit, energy and intelligence. It staged 34 sell-out shows featuring playwrights like David Greig, folk-singers like Dick Gaughan, comedians like Keir MacAllister, and writers talking about whatever happened to take their interest. One event featured a lecture on town planning. There were echoes in the Yestival of late John McGrath's 7:84 company which took the satirical review, *The Cheviot, the Stag and the Black Black Oil* around village halls in the Highlands in the 1970s.

Yestivals aside, many of National Collective's initiatives were frankly naïve. They aroused derision in some quarters for their wish trees, maps, flash fiction, knitting groups, and guerrilla cinema. Some of the poetry published by National Collective was poor. Some bemused press commentators like David Torrance dismissed independence creatives as amateurish, agitprop, simplistic, and ill-informed. There is something in that of course, but it rather missed the point. The Collective wasn't about trying to appeal to the arts establishment, win Turner Prizes or get grants from Creative Scotland. Nor did it fit its portrayal as a crowd of gushing indy luvvies in the West End of Glasgow, or at Edinburgh Festival Yurts. It was a new form of political organisation primarily about mobilising peoples' imaginations to build support for independence and counter its negative portrayal in the conventional media. Its naiveté was part of its strength because it allowed practically anyone who felt they had something to say to get involved. As *The Herald*'s arts correspondent Phil Miller explained, National Collective "represents the foundation of something new in Scotland, and long-needed, a collective, grassroots voice for and from the artistic world not tethered to existing institutions."

Even the hard-headed *Economist* eventually got it: "Colour benefits the 'yes' campaign. It generates an infectious energy, as some senior Unionists quietly admit. Nationalists are "like religious believers", whispers one, both mocking and impressed. And energy means the independence movement has more contact with voters". "If the "no" campaign is a machine, "yes" is a carnival", said Fraser Nelson in *The Spectator*, noting that the No campaign had been "dismal, colourless, negative and crassly economistic, seeking to value the Union at £1,400 per head or 10 weeks of fish suppers".

THE WRITERS' REFERENDUM

The Herald commentator David Torrance not only dismissed National Collective as juvenile but condemned the literary Yes community as empty-headed. "Most writers' interventions in the independence debate (on both sides)", he wrote, "have betrayed the worst sort of naive, ill-informed analysis worthy of student politics. There are honourable exceptions, but not many. Levels of sanctimoniousness have also gone through the roof". Well, the roll call of the honourable exceptions included Irvine Welsh, William McIlvanney, the late Iain Banks, Christopher Brookmyre, Alasdair Gray, James Robertson, James Kelman, David Greig, Liz Lochhead, AL Kennedy, Val McDiarmid, Alan Warner, Kathleen Jamie, Sara Sheridan. The list goes on and on.

If this was student politics, then the university of the referendum was a pretty interesting place. Scotland's greatest living historian Professor Sir Tom Devine also spoke for Yes and he was not alone in university life: over sixty academics launched Academics For Yes in February 2014. And literary figures didn't just sign letters of support but used their talents to campaign in their own ways. There have been initiatives in the past like Red Wedge and Rock Against Racism that have tried to marry politics and pop music. But I can't think of a time when so many established writers were prepared to get their hands dirty in the sordid business of politics. In fact, almost the entire Scottish literary community seemed to turn to independence practically overnight in the Summer of 2014.

I was at a packed event at the Ullapool Book Festival in May when the celebrated Scottish novelist William McIlvanney declared that he was going to vote Yes. The author of the *Laidlaw* books had been a massive presence in the Labour-led campaign for a Scottish Parliament in the 1980s and 90s and his decision now to back independence – despite having been a long term critic of small-minded nationalism – was a significant cultural event. He was one of the few writers that Better Together didn't try to rubbish as a "luvvie".

McIlvanney, son of a miner, bone fide man of the people, and arguably one of the most gifted writers Scotland has ever produced, practically embodies the values of the Scottish labour movement. His books vividly presented Scottish working-class culture to working people in a manner which has made them best sellers over generations. Willie had always been a Labour man, through and through, but in Ullapool he said, more in sorrow than in anger: "Labour's all shop window, now – there's nothing in the back shop. This is Scotland's last chance." He said he wanted to "call Scotland's bluff". Is Scotland really this social democratic, communitarian culture where social justice is more important than personal enrichment? he asked. Now was the moment to discover whether it was true.

Not everyone in the literary world was persuaded of the merits of independence. McIlvanney's literary alter ego, the Harry Potter novelist JK Rowling, made a high profile intervention in the referendum campaign with a heart-felt appeal to Scots to stay in the Union. She is a long-time Labour supporter and appended to her June 2014 "letter" was a £1 million donation so that Better Together didn't have to rely on crowdfunding. Nevertheless, JK Rowling's appeal, published on 10th June 2014, was well written, considered, and undoubtedly struck a chord with many Scottish voters, especially women who regarded the nationalist movement and Alex Salmond with great suspicion, and thought the Yes Campaign, while full of optimism, was hopelessly naïve about the risks of independence. Rowling cited independent authorities including the Institute for Fiscal Studies, which she said had warned about the possibility of an independent Scotland's ageing population leading to a structural spending deficit. She also cited *Scotland's Choices* written by prominent Unionist academics, Professors Iain McLean, Guy Lodge, and Jim Gallagher, which had warned against an independent Scotland depending on depleting oil and gas revenues.

Having concluded that independence was a pretty risky business, it was not difficult for Rowling to reject it. Since the economic case for independence was, she believed, unsupportable, that left only what she called the ethnic nationalist case. "When people try to make this debate about the purity of your lineage" she went on, "things start getting a little death eaterish for my taste". It wasn't clear who the death eaters actually were – again when nationalism is involved there is a kind of unspoken assumption that it must somehow be about race. However, Rowling insisted that she was not a dyed-in-the wool Unionist and was only voting No because she was sure Westminster would deliver "devolution max". "My guess is that if we vote to stay, we will be in the heady position of the spouse who looked like walking out, but decided to give things one last go". Marital metaphors were very much part of the Unionist platform: divorce is a costly business. Mind you, sometimes remaining in a dysfunctional relationship can be costlier.

Rowling's intervention elicited an angry response from so-called "cybernats" on the internet who called her many unpleasant names. This was hugely damaging because it allowed the press to portray the independence supporters as death-eaters incarnate. Unionists like the Labour blogger John McTernan accused the Yes Campaign on STV's *Scotland Tonight* (12/6/14) of "organising a co-ordinated campaign of hate" against Rowling. This was without foundation, but the newspapers reproduced the abusive and sexist tweets and left it for their readers to judge. They didn't do the same for the many Scottish female celebrities on the other side who received similar treatment, like Elaine C Smith, or Nicola Sturgeon, the Deputy First Minister, who found herself a target, not just of sexist and abusive hate-tweets, but actual death threats.

While the press recycled vituperative comments on the internet against Rowling, they did not find space for a considered response from the Scottish academic Mairi McFadyen on behalf of National Collective:

> The campaign you see is not the campaign I see. I see a generation of people who are not afraid, who speak articulately, passionately about the possibilities of a better future. I am struck on a daily basis by the goodwill, kindness, open-mindedness, generosity, intelligence, creativity, humility and sheer dedication of all of those giving their everything to this movement. My own involvement has been one of the most humbling and inspiring experiences of my life. Of course, we don't all agree on our political vision, but we do have one thing in common: we have the desire to work together towards a better future.

This almost evangelical optimism of the Yes campaign was derided by many Unionist writers, including Carol Craig, author of *The Tears that Made the Clyde*. She wrote a companion piece to Rowling's letter for *Scottish Review*, which was also reproduced extensively in the press. It condemned "Project Pollyanna", as she described the Yes campaign, with its constant accentuation of the positive. This was somewhat ironic because Craig is director of a charity called The Scottish Centre for Confidence and Wellbeing, which seeks to apply the ideas of the "positive thinking" guru Martin Seligman to counter Scotland's alleged lack of confidence about itself and its capacities. She even published a book called *The Scots' Crisis of Confidence*. But this was the wrong kind of confidence, said Craig, and didn't accept the reality that becoming independent in a harsh world would be risky. "The great crash" she argued in *The Guardian*, "taught us just how vulnerable economies can be. Indeed the economies of Ireland, Iceland, Spain and Greece almost toppled under the weight of the resultant debt". The economies of Norway, Denmark, Finland and Switzerland didn't of course, but, like most Unionists, Carol Craig believes it is self-evident that an independent Scotland would be a financial basket case because it depends on subsidies from London and lacks a fully developed national economy. So keep a hold of nurse for fear of something worse. And of course, she added, hadn't Orwell warned about nationalism...

One of the reasons JK Rowling's intervention made such an impact was that it was so rare. Very few Unionist writers or artists in Scotland, or England, chose to raise their heads above the parapet. There was no unionist equivalent of National Collective, for example. There was really only one significant cultural event, *The Spectator*-promoted Unity rally in Trafalgar Square right at the very end of the campaign. That brought together figures like Eddie Izzard, Bob Geldof and the Scottish writer Jenny Colgan. But this slightly backfired when Colgan, the author of *Operation Sunshine,* condemned the "flaccid No campaign" with its "focus on the dry, the... tedious the scaremongering" and wondered aloud why "the Yesses have had all the fun". [19] Hugo Rifkind wistfully wrote in *The Times* of his regret that, as a No voter, the colour seemed to have drained from the Union: "All the magic has been surrendered, and so feebly, to the other side", he said, wondering why the UK seemed unable to inspire artists and writers in the way the independence movement clearly had. Partly this was because Better Together tended to dismiss all this arty stuff as a bit of a joke, and a diversion from "getting oot the vote". But that doesn't quite explain why the many Unionist artists, intellectuals, and performers didn't do some creative space clearing of their own.

One "grassroots" cultural campaign which received much attention, at least on the BBC, was 'Vote No Borders'. Supposedly established spontaneously by concerned Scottish citizens, this produced a website, some songs and an advertising campaign. The human rights activist Craig Murray exposed VNB as a London-based marketing campaign financed by a prominent Conservative donor, Malcolm Offord, and a PR consultant called Fiona Gilmour.[20] That perhaps would have been excusable had there been any real signs of grassroots involvement in Scotland itself in the project, or anything more substantial than a few advertising jingles and one rather derivative music video, 'Why Build Another Wall'. But the campaign always had an air of contrivance. And it lost most of its credibility when a cinema advert had to be pulled because it claimed that Scottish children would be denied treatment in Great Ormond Street Hospital after independence.

There were a number of individual artists and performers who opposed independence, like Sharlene Spiteri of Texas, comedians like Billy Connolly (though even he declared in the end that he was "neutral"), artists like David Shrigley, Martin Creed, and classical composer James MacMillan. Anecdotally, it seemed that a very large number of people involved in classical music and opera in Scotland were opposed to independence, perhaps out of fear of the bagpipes. The composer Eddie McGuire wrote Unity Suite as a cultural contribution to the Better Together campaign. But the vast majority chose not to declare their intentions, or said they had no views, like the violinist Nicola Benadetti. Writers like John Burnside, Ian Rankin, and Alexander McCall Smith, also remained silent and it was inferred from their political affiliations that they were No voters.

But why were there were no Unionist umbrella campaigns like National Collective? Jenny Hjul in the *Daily Telegraph* suggested it was because they were afraid they might be might be accused of being anti-Scottish and be pursued by abusive "cybernats".[21] Jenny Colgan complained of being pursued by "McTrolls – Jings, I wouldn't let those bawheids look after a hamster never mind a newborn state". The BBC Radio Scotland DJ Tom Morton suggested some Unionists feared for their careers: "a number of people on that scene have told me they fear going public on their No stance because of the potential repercussions". It isn't clear what these would be since there was certainly no restriction on Unionist voices in the Scottish press or the BBC. Quite the reverse. Anyone who did speak up, like Jenny Colgan or even Vote No Borders, was guaranteed a sympathetic hearing and wide exposure in the mainstream media.But this is anyway a feeble explanation – when have artists and writers been so timid that they would be put off expressing their view of the world by a few juvenile twits on the internet? The Yes Campaign had to put up with continual assaults for being Nazis in literally thousands of tweets like these:

Sep 16
Scotland are shit anyway they've only got andy murray an hes a wanker fuck Scotland and fuck murray

Sep 17
#SNP = Scottish Nazi (Nationalist Socialist) Party. They & many supporters are authoritarian, bigoted, aggressive, incoherent, deceitful.

Sep 16
.@AlexSalmond Your a fucking fat oaf. At least if you go independent your future diet of nettles and rabbit will help you lose a few pounds.

Perhaps the very reason there was no Artists For No campaign was because they took this taint of fascism seriously. The composer, James MacMillan contributed to this general portrayal of the Yes campaign as essentially fascist in an article in *The Scotsman* where he gave the reasons why he thought artists were not coming out and speaking in favour of the Union.[22] He dismissed National Collective as "young, shouty and completely unquestioning about their cause... producing propaganda rather than art" which is a perfectly legitimate criticism to make, though there is a difference between committed art and agitprop. However he went on to say that it is unwise in principle to "tie art to belief", which is an interesting if depressing proposition. MacMillan then devoted half his article to suggestion that the Yes campaign must be suspect because a former SNP member, the poet Hugh MacDiarmid, was a "Nazi sympathiser", which is untrue. He was actually a Communist, but never mind. It is absurd to dismiss a movement, artistic or political, because the objectionable attitudes of a former supporter.

I am genuinely puzzled about why there wasn't any collective engagement by Scottish creatives wanting to support the United Kingdom. *The Guardian*'s Jonathan Jones, a Welshman, called for one. "Nationalism is a cultural black hole. It leads to small-mindedness" he wrote, "not to the generous utopia that leftwing Scottish "yes" voters dream of... Scotland's art is doing brilliantly as an inflection of British art." It was understandable that English artists felt inhibited about bigging up the Union in Scotland. But there has been a raft of Scottish Turner Prize Winners like Douglas Gordon, Richard Wright and Martin Boyce who are opposed to independence, and were prepared individually to express their view. But they didn't get it together collectively. Perhaps this was because when artists become successful they generally leave Scotland and lose interest in domestic politics. Wendy McMurdo, one of the "Glasgow" generation of artists and an opponent of independence told *The Guardian*:

The majority of successful artists depend on an international network of curators and galleries to advance their careers and to give them the exposure beyond the countries they choose to live in.

She went on: "Certainly for me, any exploration of identity cannot – should not – be limited to the national." There is a suggestion that only artists whose horizons were limited to Scotland were motivated to enter into this arena. But this was a curious explanation for the failure of artists like McMurdo to join in an existential debate about the destiny of the country of their birth. Did nobody think to ask them?

There was nothing to be ashamed of in supporting unity and togetherness, or backing the United Kingdom. Britain is not a communist dictatorship or an oppressive regime. It is one of the oldest democracies in the world. It leads the world in popular culture, if not high culture. There is surely inspiration to be had in the history of a great partnership, the UK, which fought fascism, created the welfare state and voluntarily gave up its empire after Harold Macmillan's Winds of Change speech in 1960. Thereafter, British fashion and popular culture dominated the world, as was celebrated with such verve and wit by Danny Boyle's opening ceremony at the 2012 Olympic games. Indeed, his colourful pageant of British achievement – the industrial revolution, chartism and dancing NHS nurses – was precisely the sort of people's history that might have reached hearts and minds in Scotland where commitment to the values of post-war social democracy remain strong. Even Alex Salmond had to agree that it was brilliant, though he felt it rather neglected Scotland's contribution to the industrial culture. Boyle's show was propaganda of a kind, but still art, of exactly the kind that might have appealed to the young internet-savvy Scots who were turning to nationalism. But instead what Better Together produced was the pantomime "love bombing" of well-meaning UK artistes like Vera Lynn, Dan Snow, Eddie Izzard, Ross Kemp, Tracey Emin. This was, at times, excruciating and patronising even if it was well intended. David Beckham said No and Vivienne Westwood backed Yes: I think we know who carries more Scottish street cred.

Unionist writers had a unique opportunity in the 2014 referendum campaign to repackage the Union and liberate it from the dry economism and banker unionism of Better Together. The press and media were eager to provide a platform for anyone willing to praise the UK as the Craig/Rowling pieces confirmed. And the UK artistic community had been here before. Back in the 1970s, during the first appearances of political Scottish nationalism, artists and intellectuals were generally suspicious of the SNP and its rather crass demands for Scotland's Oil. Many of them believed that nationalists were essentially sectarian bigots. Even John McGrath of 7:84 insisted that he wasn't a nationalist, even though *The Cheviot* came to be regarded as an SNP review. What then worried many intellectuals, especially in Scottish universities, was the prospect of being cut-off from the great history of English letters: Shakespeare, the Romantic poets, Defoe, Dickens, Woolf and cultural institutions like Royal Shakespeare Company. All Scotland had to offer was a parochial, tartan culture of Brigadoon, or so they said. Who would choose Jimmy Shand and his band when you could have Elgar? It hardly needs to be said that those critics of Scottish provincialism were only demonstrating their own philistinism by ignoring the work of the country that produced Burns, Scott, Stevenson, Conan Doyle, Collins, Buchan, and MacDiarmid himself.

THE FALL OF THE BBC

In the 1970s, during the devolution debates, the Labour MP Brian Wilson used to condemn nationalists for wanting to exchange the BBC for The White Heather Club, a cringe-worthy country dancing show transmitted in the 1950s and 60s. The presumption was that Scotland could never afford the David Attenboroughs and the Lord Clarks who made the BBC internationally renowned as "the greatest broadcasting organisation in the world". Any independent Scottish broadcaster would be reduced to churning out cheap local shows of little cultural value. The BBC used to be an absolute pillar of cultural unionism, and until recently the thought of dismantling it would have seemed almost like sacrilege. But not any more, it seems.

When Lord Birt the former BBC Direcror General, told *The Guardian* in August 2014 that independence would have a "devastating impact" on the corporation, and that Scottish viewers would no longer have access to much of its output, the reaction was distinctly muted.[23] The Yes Campaign pointed out that people can watch all the BBC channels in independent Ireland. The reaction on social media was: so what? Any threat to the BBC in the past would have aroused an angry response in Scotland from middle-class intellectuals and the general public worried about parochialism. Perhaps, in today's multi-channel, digital environment, the threat to withdraw *Strictly Come Dancing, The Great British Bake Off* and *Doctor Who* doesn't pack quite the same punch as in the great days of *House of Cards* and Denis Potter. The best drama on television today comes not from the BBC but from subscription stations in the US like HBO, which made *The Wire*, or from small countries in the North of Europe, like Denmark's *Borgen* and *The Killing*.

The BBC had also been through a succession of damaging scandals. The overpayment of current and former BBC executives was criticised by the press and a Commons committee. The Jimmy Savile affair had also tarnished the reputation of the corporation when it emerged that the entertainer had abused many of his victims on BBC premises. The BBC also became a casualty of the propaganda wars in the referendum campaign. There was, and is, a very profound belief among many supporters of independence in Scotland that the corporation sought to demonise nationalism, be disrespectful to the First Minister and undermine the Yes campaign.

Some of the BBC news coverage was certainly ham-fisted as I explore in the next chapter. And *Question Time*, though produced in Glasgow, hardly seems to be aware that it is transmitted in Scotland, so frequently are figures like Nigel Farage invited onto their panels without comparable representation from Scottish nationalists. There is also the perennial problem of the BBC's network news bulletins featuring stories about health and education that are not relevant in Scotland because of devolution – a problem that should have been remedied fifteen years ago by the creation of a Scottish Six O'Clock News. The BBC's own King Report in 2008 identified a metropolitan bias in its news and current affairs.

But the BBC did at least allow its business editor, Robert Peston, to produce a remarkably positive assessment of Scotland's economic potential in *Scotland: For Richer; For Poorer* at a key moment in the referendum campaign. And the Scottish output from correspondents like Brian Taylor and James Cook was above reproach. It was actually Channel 4 who invited the right-wing Conservative MP Jacob Rees Mogg to tour Scotland and patronise its inhabitants – though it seems to have gone down in nationalist mythology as a BBC ploy. Mind you, Mogg's encounter with young Dundonians on their way to get their methadone prescriptions was classic television and probably handed the Yes campaign a few more votes.

So, why was there quite so much animosity towards the BBC? Well, partly because the BBC's news and current affairs shows tend to take their cue from the agenda of the newspapers, which, as I explain in the next chapter were markedly pro-Unionist. It didn't handle issues like the relocation of banking jobs well; Nick Robinson was caught out selectively editing the First Minister. But the problem goes deeper. Broadcasting has also lost much of its mystique in the age of the multi-channel internet and Youtube. You can watch amateurs doing television now in homespun ventures such as Referendum TV. Nowadays, people don't like to be talked down to by figures of authority, whether in Westminster or on the BBC. James Robertson's poem, 'The News Where You Are', which became a standard at Yes events, summed this up very well. It wickedly satirised the patronising, top-down attitude of metropolitan news bulletins.

In many ways the decline of the BBC came to represent, in microcosm, the cultural decline of he United Kingdom itself. Culture has become fragmented in the last forty years and is no longer as monolithic, elitist, metropolitan as it was in the 1970s. Indeed, the great tradition of English literature is not what it was, having got lost in chick lit and fifty shades of pornography. The art of Tracey Emin's unmade bed or Damien Hirst's bling skull speak of little apart from sensationalism, solipsism, and excess. Also with the demystifying of elite culture, people have been invited to go out and make their own art, and many have been doing that in Scotland. We live in an age defined by the collapse of deference, and organisations like National Collective are part of a radical social-democratic movement which deferred to no one, whether of the left or in the artistic establishment. People in Scotland still watch BBC programmes, of course, and the SNP recognised this by calling, in the White Paper on independence, for a joint venture with the Scottish Broadcasting Service after independence. But people in Scotland have moved, younger voters in particular, into the multichannel digital age. Too many Unionist politicians were still living in the analogue past when the BBC was a kind of cultural priesthood.

POLLYANNA VERSUS LENIN

But did all this optimistic Pollyanna stuff make any difference? Better Together won after all. Didn't the Yes Campaign lose out to a conventional professional political machine? As Blair McDougall, the campaign chief of Better Together famously put it: "you don't win elections by sitting on bean bags reciting poetry". The nearest BT got to poetry was their TV advertising campaign, which was was defined by one ad that became known as "Patronising BT Lady", and was lampooned across the internet. The lady in question couldn't recall the name of the First Minister and said there weren't "enough hours in the day" to be bothering about politics. Many women found this not just patronising but positively offensive. BT said it was based on what women were saying to their canvassers on the doorsteps; it was how "real" women saw the referendum.

There were many conventionally-minded politicians even in the SNP who regarded the activities of the cultural groups like National Collective with, if not contempt, then certainly some scepticism. There was always a feeling that this wasn't quite serious politics; that poetry didn't persuade. The former deputy leader of he SNP, Jim Fairlie, told *The Scotsman* (23/10/14) that the Yes campaign wasn't reaching the middle-classes. Nor did everyone believe in the power of the web. The former Yes Campaign executive Susan Stewart argued in *Strategem*:

> The digital and social media campaign... failed to persuade undecided or No-leaning women. Nor were the majority of over 60s convinced. Much has been written about the power of the internet in this referendum but it can also be an echo chamber, serving only to confirm the 'true believers' in the rightness of their cause. (24/9/14)

There is an argument that if the Yes campaign had spent less time dreaming and more canvassing it might actually have won over that lost 5% that made the difference between 45% and independence. Many insiders in the Yes Campaign have told me of their regret that more effort was not put into gathering voter intelligence and early canvassing. The suggestion is that the cultural cadres may have been having a great time but they were largely preaching to the converted and not getting the message across to middle-class voters, seniors and women.

On the other hand, organisations like the SNP and Radical Independence were supposed to be doing much of that rather effectively anyway. I'm not sure that the cultural campaign was as ineffectual as might appear. Because here's the thing – in the weekends since the referendum, the losers began staging what almost look like celebrations, with thousands of independence supporters holding mass rallies outside the Scottish Parliament and in Glasgow city centre. These people just didn't want to give up. Normally a defeat in an election leads to a period of cultural and political defeatism and negativity. But the Yes campaign simply carried on, with organisations like Common Weal, National Collective and Bella Caledonia increasing their membership and their resources. This is surely the power of culture and art, that engages people emotionally and spiritually and not just as an electoral army trying to win an election. This was the crucial difference, for me certainly, between the referendum campaign and the many election campaigns I have been involved in before. People felt genuinely transformed by their experience of the campaign.

It was less the actual content of the cultural activity but more its inclusive character that was important. National Collective and other organisations created a very potent contemporary democratic myth: the possibility that through popular engagement, it is possible to create a better, more socially just, society. Not just as a set of manifesto promises, but as a practical, conscious activity. Even the much-maligned wish trees were remarkably successful in allowing non-political people to make political statements. Some of the contributions were very moving. There was a sense of ownership of the referendum campaign, which helped people who were alienated from all conventional politics to become involved and active. The cultural dimension also contributed enormously to the morale of the independence campaign.

The referendum was the first time I can recall in Britain when artists and writers really were in the forefront of a political movement and not just ornaments to it. There were echoes here clearly of the civic nationalist movements in central European countries before the collapse of communism – not that I would compare the UK to the Soviet Union. However, the monolithic quality of the media coverage engendered that sense of intellectual alienation which makes people look to writers and artists to articulate their feelings. The distinguished writer and journalist Neal Ascherson said he saw more than echoes of the popular movements he had seen first hand in Eastern and Central Europe: "In the dark years before the Velvet Revolution in Czechoslovakia, Vaclav Havel used to say: 'We don't need to wait for it. Let's start living in truth now – right now. Let's live 'as if'.'" And the Polish workers, before there was Solidarity, said "Let's create spaces – authentic spaces in which a real Poland exists, in which we talk openly, wait for no permission, design our own future." As I have made clear, Scotland does not live under communist tyranny, or indeed any tyranny – but these comparisons do make sense nevertheless, even though the stakes here were lower. The cultural community started to open up those spaces in imaginative dialogue with the Scottish people who were looking for somewhere – anywhere – they could think without being bombarded by the negative messages of Project Fear.

No amount of canvassing can do this. The Yes campaign's apparently simple-minded optimism was in some ways its secret weapon. It allowed it to reach parts of the body politic that ordinary machine politics simply cannot. Or the conventional media, which in most cases simply recycled the risk agenda of the UK financial and political establishment while demonising the Yes campaign, as at best, Alex Salmond's useful idiots, and at worst, "cybernats" spreading hate. The Yes campaign had to find a way to communicate through the noise and negativity. It did this by targeting the imagination, especially, but by no means exclusively, of younger Scots who had already largely given up on the conventional media in favour of the internet.

The Yes campaign clearly won the argument among the young and the less affluent, but it did so not by rousing class anger, which has been the traditional rallying cry of the radical left, but by inspiring people with a vision of what could be a better society. One of the refreshing things about the 2014 independence campaigning was the lack of the austere Marxist dialectic which dominated nearly all radical politics in the second half of the last century. It did not resort to the language of class enemies. The Yes campaign did not speak about leading the working-class to revolution, as if they were a herd of sheep needing to be guided by Leninist ideologues. Nor did Yes supporters have to sit still while Marxist intellectuals talked down to them, criticising their thinking, laughing at their reformist illusions and telling them to join study groups in historical materialism. The ideology of the Yes campaign was eclectic, socialist, pacifist, and sometimes confused, but it was invariably inclusive and democratic. If its head was sometimes a bit lost it always knew where its heart lay.

The Yes campaign managed to mobilise huge numbers peacefully and without any democratic centralist party or organisation machine. By allowing the people to make it their own, the campaign unleashed creative energy that was self-sustaining – it didn't need party discipline. This also meant that the movement did not get lost in the internal factionalism that has been the downfall of all vanguardist parties of the left. There were far left people involved, especially in the Radical Independence Campaign, but they never dominated it. The Socialist Workers Party kept its head down and there was no sign of Class War or any of the anarchist groups who turn up at mass meetings to counsel confrontation. Instead there were plays, poems, songs, wish trees and people talking about dreams of a better nation.

The losers in the Scottish referendum felt they were the winners. They acted as winners because they had rehearsed it in their imagination. The continuing strength of the independence movement, as the referendum recedes, owes a great deal to the artists who helped Scotland re-imagine itself. As Ian Bell put it in *The Herald*:

> A popular movement permeates a society; a manufactured campaign buys software, consultants and volunteers as required... Yes, the world knows, has all the best tunes. It has the best jokes, the best slogans, the best speeches. Of Scots, it has the best writers, historians, actors, lawyers, painters, doctors, farmers, politicians, constitutional theorists, political thinkers, and more. It has a buzz, a sense of commitment and belief, a work rate. Above all, it has a grassroots campaign that Better Together, wedded to cynicism and a template from a box stamped 'Quebec', cannot match... It has been infused with an optimism and a belief that ought to bounce from my calloused hide like

most of the 'inspirational' noise summoned up by paid campaign directors... It has been a campaign without precedent in these islands.[24]

However, while the cultural cadres of the Yes campaign were winning the war on the ground and in social media, they lost very badly in the air war in the mainstream media, which was still dominated by a press which refused to be moved by all the poetry. The Yes campaign's conventional press management wasn't so much poor as non-existent.

CHAPTER FOUR

The Press We Deserve – Unionism and the Mainstream Media

The week before Easter 2014, the editor of the *Sunday Herald*, Richard Walker, gathered his staff at the Renfield Street headquarters of Newsquest Herald and Times. It only required a small conference room. 'God, is this all that's left of us?' I thought, as I sat down with colleagues on the paper I had been writing for since its birth in 1999. I knew there had been ruthless staff cuts in order to keep the *Sunday Herald* alive, but it was a shock nevertheless to realise that one of Scotland's most influential organs of news and comment was produced by about seventeen people.

Walker had already made up his mind to back independence after sounding out staff individually, and he wasn't putting it to a vote. But all had had a chance to speak at this meeting. My only concern was that, for tactical reasons if nothing else, we should wait until it was clear that the Unionist parties had failed to come up with a coherent plan for federalism, as some had been suggesting they might. He was anxious not to be upstaged by other papers that also might be thinking of being the first to back a Yes in the referendum. Well, that was one thing he needn't have worried about.

I was surprised by the enthusiasm of the *Sunday Herald* staff for taking this independent line. It was one of the earliest indications that the Yes campaign really had reached the parts the Unionist campaign had not. It tended to be the younger members of the *Sunday Herald* team who seemed most up for it. The news reporters were understandably concerned about the possibility that stories hostile to Alex Salmond would be spiked. They were assured that they would not be. There were also fears expressed around the table that stories might dry up if the *Sunday Herald* was black-balled by Labour – an indication that, though Labour had been out of power for seven years, the tribe still held on to many key positions in Scottish public life. This was a risky step any way you looked at it. Newspapers usually wait until near polling day to declare their positions, for very good reasons. They don't want to be on the losing side and risk antagonising readers and losing sales. Traditionally, newspapers wait until it's clear where public opinion is headed and then claim to be leading it, as *The Sun* did so famously in the 1980s and 90s. Yet at this stage, the Yes campaign was in the doldrums and no one seemed to give independence the remotest chance of victory. Unionist Labour bloggers like Ian Smart were predicting that Yes would return less than 30% of the vote in the referendum. Psephologists like Professor John Curtice of Strathclyde University were saying that time was running out for Yes. The US election guru, Nat Silver, had said a Yes vote was almost a statistical impossibility.

Everyone in that room, from the editor down, realised that this was a very serious step that could affect the future of the paper and everyone writing for it. Being on the wrong side might have not only undermined the *Sunday Herald*'s credibility, it could have blighted the careers of people working for it. Scottish journalism is almost as tribal as Scottish politics, and Labour has traditionally called the shots in the Scottish media through its extensive patronage networks. The top-selling *Daily Record* used to be a Labour donor.[25] However, what swung the argument wasn't stories or sales or image but the responsibility of the paper to Scottish civil society. It sounds pompous, but the *Sunday Herald* took its role in the democratic process very seriously.

We all realised, whatever our views, that it would simply be a perversion of that process if all newspapers supported the Union. Any experienced journalist could see that the rest of the Scottish and UK press were making their editorial positions clear day by day on their front pages in the prominence they gave to negative stories about independence, even though they hid behind a thin cloak of editorial neutrality. We felt, on the contrary, that we should level with our readers, and say where we stood clearly from the outset. And to give credit to Newsquest, the proprietors of the *Sunday Herald* stood back from this process and left their editors with the freedom they needed to decide on their own positions. Newsquest is a UK publishing company with American owners and has often been criticised in recent years, by Unions and by MSPs, for its commercialism and its staff cuts – but no one could criticise its commitment to independent journalism.

And so, on 3rd May, to catcalls and jeers from Scottish journalists on Twitter, the *Sunday Herald* ran a striking front page designed by Alasdair Gray, and declared its stance in the referendum. Almost immediately, the *Sunday Herald* was attacked as "Pravda", a propaganda sheet for the SNP. I got used to being called a "nat spin-doctor" by Scottish journalists who affected to be neutral but were as partisan as the *Daily Mail*. Among the many names I was called the one I liked best was "Iain Natwhirter". It was futile to point out that I was not and never had been a member of the SNP and didn't even describe myself as a nationalist. The tribalism that has long afflicted Scottish politics is also evident in the Scottish media. Some of my oldest friends and many people I admire in journalism took profound personal offence and told me I had become "a bitter propagandist". There was a presumption that taking a broad Unionist line was in some way the impartial and objective way to approach the referendum.

So, it wasn't a particularly pleasant time. But I can't think of a moment when I felt more proud of being part of my dismal trade than when I opened my historic copy of the *Sunday Herald*. The editorial had been written by Richard Walker, distilling the views of the writers and editors. This is what it said:

> We view the referendum not as a choice between the status quo and an uncertain future, but as between a bankrupt, political structure and the chance to remake our society in a more equal, inclusive, open and just way. A referendum cannot immediately wash away the legacy of the past. September's vote is not a straight choice between that past and an already-formed future. What is offered is the chance to alter course, to travel roads less taken, to define a destiny.
>
> Some newspapers are against independence, others merely unsympathetic to the notion. We do not believe this to be healthy. Scotland's media should reflect the diversity of opinion within the country. We believe that in a real democracy the public should have access to a wide range of views and opinions. The media should not speak with one voice.
>
> Diversity of opinion is reflected within the *Sunday Herald*'s staff. Some of our team support independence, some do not, and others are still considering the arguments. Some are unconvinced by the merits of supporting a Yes vote. Far from regarding this as a weakness, we welcome it. The *Sunday Herald* has always been a broad church. We consider the fact a strength which we will always protect.

And we will continue to seek the views of Better Together to maintain balance in our news stories. Clearly we do not share the views of the No campaign but we respect their right to their opinion and believe that they are as passionate about Scotland's future as we are. This is not an argument which should be mired in personal hatred.

Scotland is an ancient nation and a modern society. We understand the past, as best we can, and guess at the future. But history is as nothing to the lives of the children being born now, this morning, in the cities, towns and villages of this country. On their behalf, we assert a claim to a better, more decent, more just future in which a country's governments will be ruled always by the decisions of its citizens. Scots have never been afraid to astonish the world. A small country has made a habit of producing big thinkers. *The Sunday Herald* says that it is time to think big once again. And to think for ourselves.

The Sunday Herald's sister paper, *The Herald*, took a different line. In a remarkable 2,000 word statement, which even referred to the Italian Marxist Antonio Gramsci, it argued that the economic case for independence had not been made.

On oil revenues, entering a currency union, achieving EU membership promptly and smoothly, securing affordable rates of interest for borrowing on the international markets and its capacity to withstand global economic currents, the case for independence has been   built upon a string of ideal outcomes.

However, it was critical of Better Together and described the Unionist campaign as "a corporate marketing department without a product to sell". *The Herald* called for "a federal UK" and ended with a warning to Westminster:

The Herald backs Scotland staying within the UK at this stage. But fudge this process, stitch it up and fail to deliver far-reaching further devolution, and make no mistake: you will be guaranteeing another referendum – one that you will lose, and deserve to lose.

Strangely, I found myself nodding in agreement even though I'd decided to vote Yes. I suspect many readers of the papers had the same experience.

I continued to write for both papers, and I was repeatedly asked how I managed to keep doing so. In fact, the question never arose because neither *The Herald*, the oldest newspaper in the English-speaking world, nor *The Sunday Herald* tell their journalists what to write. Yet many people I spoke to, even in the Yes campaign, seemed to be under the impression that these were monolithic editorial positions that required absolute obedience. But this wasn't an exercise in thought control. I was at no time urged to skew anything I wrote to fit with any editorial line.

Happily for the proprietors of the *Sunday Herald*, this was one of the occasions when editorial open-mindedness was rewarded with commercial success. *The Sunday Herald*'s circulation immediately began to rise after its declaration and by the week before the referendum its sales had more than doubled. This is all the more remarkable given that newspapers in general have been losing sales at a rate of nearly 10% a year as readers cross over to tablets and laptops.

Richard Walker's decision to support independence early was the right one, giving the paper a clear identity and more importantly giving the Scottish voters some degree of choice at the news stands. Arguably, the success of the *Sunday Herald* underlines the extent to which they were not being given that choice. It always seemed curious that, for marketing reasons if nothing else, no newspaper in Scotland had supported independence (except, briefly, *The Sun* in 1992). *The Irish Independent* sells more than twice as many copies as *The Herald* in a similar-sized market. It probably has as much to do with the fact that the papers that dominate the Scottish market tend to be southern-owned.

A PARTISAN PRESS

The rest of the UK Scottish press remained firmly Unionist, though most didn't declare openly until the final week of the campaign. But "Blow for Salmond" became a standing joke among journalists in Scotland because of the regularity with which it appeared on the front pages. The press coverage consistently equated the Yes campaign with the personality of the First Minister and led to the negative, emphasising risk, uncertainty, and the lack of a so-called "plan B" for the currency of an independent Scotland. Day by day, the front pages featured headlines about mortgage rates rising, pensions being cut, exclusion from the EU and other "indyscares" as they became known, while the positive case for independence rarely made it to the news pages. Some prominent Yes-supporting columnists, like Lesley Riddoch and the former SNP MSP Andrew Wilson, were given space however on the inside pages.

Editors get very defensive when they are accused of being partisan, muttering about censorship and intimidation and insisting that they follow independent editorial guidelines. And many do. They understandably resent any suggestion that there wasn't fair play in the referendum, the most important political event in Scotland in three hundred years, and insist that they reported the campaign as they found it. But editors and journalists are very much of-the-day people, and they tend to suffer from a kind of selective amnesia. They rarely look dispassionately at their collective output as a whole to see the overall message their headlines are conveying. But it was abundantly clear to any general reader that the Scottish and UK press was hostile to independence.

It would be a huge task to go through each story individually, but fortunately we don't have to. Throughout the referendum campaign, the independent PR agency Press Data provided its 400 clients in Scotland with a daily summary of the biggest stories in the campaign in its email round robin called 'Referendum Daily'. Press Data assigned these stories on a daily ranking, highlighting the top six or seven that had dominated the front pages and page leads across the thirty odd daily and weekly titles that have significant sales in Scotland – *The Scotsman*, *The Herald*, *The Guardian*, the *Daily Mail*, *The Times* etc. The journalists on Press Data were not part of any campaign, had no axe to grind and are completely independent. I contacted them myself to ask about how they compiled their summaries. They insisted that they tried to present as balanced a picture as possible. However, their job was not to impose any political balance from without, but to reflect, honestly and comprehensively, the stories that were making the news on any particular day.

Press Data's daily summaries provide a useful picture therefore of the overall balance of the referendum coverage throughout the crucial weeks between 5th August, when the campaign got underway after the Commonwealth Games, and polling day on 18th September. As can be seen from the headlines, printed in the appendix, negative stories dominate overall by around three to one. As far as the very top stories of the day are concerned, the ones really that made the news, the ratio was nearly four to one in favour of the Unionist point of view.

By negative stories, I do not merely refer those with hostile quotes about Alex Salmond, the SNP or independence. I mark as No only those stories whose top lines significantly undermined the key arguments and the morale of the Yes campaign: such as banks threatening to leave Scotland, oil reserves running out, food prices rising, threats of exclusion from NATO, the sterling zone, and the European Union. Actually many of the stories marked Yes carried a hostile spin, such as Alex Salmond's criticism of the BBC or his "Declaration of Arbroath", which was seen by many papers as autocratic. But I have classed them as Yes. Nor did the Press Data summaries actually recycle the often hysterical headlines about "savage racialism" (*Daily Mail*), "fear and loathing" (*Independent*), and 'lies smears and intimidation" (*Daily Telegraph*) attributed in my view unfairly to the Yes campaign. Some stories were patently ridiculous, as in the suggestion that marriages could break up as a result of the referendum and may actually have benefited the Yes campaign. Those that offered benefit to neither side or equally were assigned Neutral. Here are four reasonably typical days.

Saturday 16th August

TOP STORIES: "Ex-PM Brown: 'Currency union worst outcome for Scotland' (G Brown tells Edin Book Festival that Scotland would be in a "neo-colonial relationship after independence"') *NO*
"Reid in warning over post-indy cuts" (Lord Reid says Scots will face worse cuts than Thatcher after independence) *NO*
"Australian PM: independence a victory for 'enemies of freedom'" (Tony Abbott quote) *NO*

OTHER STORIES: "Swinney under pressure to apologise for claims of discussion with BoE" *NO*
"Scots islands to get more support" (UK Government plans for more support for islands) *NO*
"Uncertainty blocking a yes vote" (7 out of 10 voters say its impossible to predict consequences of indy in universities study)

"Academics for Yes on currency" (letter from Professor Andrew Cumbers et al.) *YES*
"SNP urge Labour to support NHS in constitution" *YES*

Saturday 30th August

TOP: "Murphy: Yes Scotland orchestrating event disruptions" (angry mobs of nationalists calling him quisling traitor, "thuggish nationalism") *NO*
"Andy Murray would represent Scotland" *YES*

OTHER: "Cameron: indy vote biggest threat to EU membership" *NO*
"Treasury chief: Falling oil and gas revenue Body Blow for Salmond" *NO*
"Clan chiefs back independence" *YES*
"Referendum Keeping Scots up at night" (Martin Aitken financial services survey say 170 clients expressed independence-related worries) *NO*

Thursday 4th September

TOP: "Union best for social justice, Miliband to say" *NO*
"Warnings for sterling stability with indy" (Goldman Sachs predict eurozone currency crisis) *NO*
"Concerns expressed over 'Yes' vote by CBI head" *NO*

OTHER: "Former Head of GCHQ expresses security concern". (Sir David Oman says SNP security and intelligence plans are seriously flawed) *NO*
"Sturgeon: Indyref mirrors 2011 victory" *YES*
"Penalty shoot out between both sides of campaign" *NEUTRAL* (Actually, the penalty shoot out turned out to be a rather good prediction of the referendum result. The Union won 5 goals to 4)

Friday 12th September

TOP: "New YouGov poll puts Better Together back in front" *NO*
"Business 'onslaught' as 90% said to be opposed to 'Yes' vote" *NO*

"Shoppers warned of higher prices after split" (John Lewis, Asda etc.) *NO*
"Brown: I'll fight Salmond – hints he'll stand as MSP" *NO*

OTHER: "North Korea Votes Yes" (Kim Jong-Un supports indy) *NO*
"Dust up in Buchanan St" *NO*

The only day when Yes actually won the headline war was the fourteenth of September, when Groundskeeper Willie of *The Simpsons*, came out for Yes.

Now, I am a journalist myself and do not criticise newspapers lightly, and as I have made clear I was a Yes voter. However, it would be hard for any reasonable person to view this material objectively and not come to the conclusion that during the referendum the press became almost an arm of the No campaign, so consistent was the promotion of negative stories about the SNP, Alex Salmond and the Yes campaign.

My analysis conforms with the only academic study conducted into the Scottish press during the referendum. In September 2014, Dundee University's "Five Million Questions" website featured an analysis by Dr David Patrick of the University of the Free State (South Africa) which used a different methodology but came to similar conclusions. Dr Patrick, who insists he was not a supporter of independence, analysed 1,578 articles in the Scottish and UK press on the referendum over the 12 months prior to the vote. He reported that "articles showing evidence of clear bias were weighted three-to-one in favour of a pro-Union position". On top stories he concluded: "headlines which did display some form of bias showed that for every headline which framed Scottish independence positively, there were 4.3 articles which were against independence". [26]

Of course, it can be argued, and has been, that the press were simply reporting the news as they found it. These were just the stories of the campaign, and it isn't the newspapers' fault either that independence was just a bad idea full of risks, or that the Yes Scotland campaign was ineffective at getting its message across. Yes Scotland's news operation undoubtedly had problems. However, there is never any "story" which is as one-sided as the story of the Scottish independence referendum appeared to be. There are always rival narratives in any political contest. As Press

Data indicate, the press tended to lead overwhelmingly with the narrative as presented by the UK political establishment – Labour, Conservative and Liberal Democrat – and responded uncritically to the claims made by banks, big business and accountancy firms.

The press did not seriously report the rival narrative: that the Westminster establishment was running a centrally-organised campaign of fear and threat; that by staying in the Union Scotland risked being taken out of the EU; that Scotland contributes more per head in taxation than the rest of the UK; that the referendum campaign was one of the most peaceful in history; that most of the links with England, such as in the NHS, would remain after independence; that Trident is an anachronistic weapon of mass destruction.

I am not saying that the negative stories were all made up or that there was conscious manipulation or distortion of news. They wouldn't have been reported by Press Data if they had been. It is obviously headline news if companies like RBS and Standard Life are threatening to relocate their head quarters even if there are no staff cuts. And of course it is news when respected think tanks like Institute For Fiscal Studies claim that an independent Scotland might have a deficit, or when top politicians say there may be obstacles to Scotland entering the EU. However, when all these stories are grouped together and repeated day-by-day, what emerges is a skewed narrative. The overall impression given was that Scotland was a country which could not stand on its own feet, would be left isolated without a currency and suffering a flight of funds and businesses.

Where was the in-depth examination of why Standard and Poor had said that an independent Scotland would have its "highest economic assessment", for example? Was it not also news that the equally respected and London-based National Institute for Economic and Social Research had pointed out that Scotland was much richer than had been reported and that the cost of providing pensions would be greatly reduced in an independent Scotland?[27] Even the *Financial Times*, which opposed independence, said that Scotland had very many economic advantages, not least the £1trillion in oil reserves in the North Sea. "Scotland has all the ingredients to be a viable nation state", it said in an assessment which I make no apologies for repeating here:

If its geographic share of UK oil and gas output is taken into account, Scotland's GDP per head is bigger than that of France. Even excluding the North Sea's hydrocarbon bounty, per capita GDP is higher than that of Italy. Oil, whisky and a broad range of manufactured goods mean an independent Scotland would be one of the world's top 35 exporters. An independent Scotland could also expect to start with healthier state finances than the rest of the UK. Although Scotland enjoys public spending well above the UK average – a source of resentment among some in England, Wales and Northern Ireland – the cost to the Treasury is more than outweighed by oil and gas revenues from Scottish waters. (13/2/14)

I'm not saying that the *Financial Times* did not have criticisms of the Yes campaign – it came out very firmly against independence. But these salient points were singularly absent from the day-to-day newspaper reportage. And I really can't understand why, because these themes would have made great front page stories. Imagine: "Scotland: richer than ever, says report"; "Pensions cheaper in an independent Scotland"; "Bankrupt Britain in the Red". A more balanced press might have reported widespread criticism of the Chancellor for unilaterally announcing that Scotland's currency, the pound, had been appropriated by the rUK – without negotiation or discussion. As I argued in Chapter Two, the pound is arguably as much Scotland's as England's since it was the product of a Union in 1707 which was supposedly a partnership of nation states, not an annexation.

Scotland was invariably compared to relatively undeveloped countries like Panama and Greece as in the use of the term "Panamisation" – a suggestion that Scotland would become something of a banana republic if it had to set up its own currency (actually the Panama banking system is the seventh most stable in the world as the Adam Smith Institute pointed out, and is in better shape than the UK's). Rarely was Scotland compared to countries like Denmark, Norway, or Finland, which have their own currencies. Credit Suisse's July 2014 report 'The Success of Small Nations' which argued that independent countries of Scotland's size were making a much better job of dealing with the challenge of globalisation than older larger states like the UK was reported. But you had to be pretty observant to see it.

To repeat: journalists did not actually falsify or invent stories – though the *Mirror*'s claim that Edinburgh's Giant Pandas might have to be sent back to China after independence teetered on the edge. It is right that papers have political stances, and these are invariably reflected in the prominence that is given to certain stories. The *Sunday Herald* tended to prominently report stories about the continuing value of North Sea Oil, for example, when other papers were invariably reporting its imminent exhaustion. But in normal elections there is usually a variety of opinions. Papers like *The Guardian* will tend to be of the left, while *The Telegraph* and the *Daily Mail* speak for the right. But in the 2014 referendum it was as if they had all suddenly become *The Telegraph*. The press pack engaged in a kind of war of escalating hyperbole, vying with each other to deliver the latest independence shock.

On the 17th September, the day before polling day, the *Daily Telegraph* ran the banner headline "Scottish referendum: Intimidation, smears and lies mar the final days". Many others said the same, pursuing a narrative based on the alleged violent behaviour of Yes campaigners, one of whom had thrown an egg at the Labour MP Jim Murphy. Never has a single egg received so many column inches. It appeared on the front pages for fully four days. Of course, politicians, even those on street corners, should not be pelted with groceries. However, the Yes Campaign's Jim Sillars was also hit by eggs – quite a number in fact. His response when they were thrown was "next time give them to a food bank, friend". Perhaps this was reported somewhere, but I certainly didn't see it.

Similarly while the novelist JK Rowling's Twitter abuse was reproduced alongside anti-English tweets, abuse of prominent nationalists seemed to get lost. There was little coverage of the numerous death threats to Salmond and Sturgeon. Between 24th January and 17th September 2014 the @BritNatAbuseBot account logged 6,500 examples of hate tweets directed at Scots and prominent nationalist politicians, none of which were reprinted in the press. Such as the following:[28]

Sep 17
If Alex Salmond was on fire and I had a hose I would wrap it around his fat neck and choke the lying bastard.

Sep 17
Nicola Sturgeon is one ugly bastard

Sep 16
A can't actually understand who would like that cow sturgeon and her wife salmond. Disgusting couple.

Sep 16
#IndyRef Can Scotland please fuck off. We don't want you —fucking leeches living off our taxes. Vote yes.

Sep 16
If Scotland leaves the Union boycott their goods. No friends with traitors. Nuke the sweaty socks. #ScotlandDecides

Sep 16
Seriously, fuck Scotland! Nothin but a bunch of ginger, haggis eatin, bagpipe blowin, kilt wearin trannies!

Yet largely on the basis of Rowling and the Murphy stories, the 2014 referendum campaign was widely reported as bitter and divisive because of the brutal and undemocratic tactics of the "cybernats" and other Yes supporters. This media trope became so widespread that the Scottish Police Federation intervened twice to try to calm things down.

On 1st September, Brian Docherty, the chair of the SPF, which represents 18,500 police in Scotland, issued a news release saying:

> The independence debate has been robust but overwhelmingly good natured and it would prove a disservice to those who have participated in it thus far to suggest that with 17 days to go, Scotland is about to disintergrate into absolute carnage on the back of making the most important decision in the country's history.

I cannot recall a situation when a police representative has actively criticised the press – even implicitly – for exaggerating the scare of public order issues. But even this warning became part of the ongoing story of street violence and intimidation and was tendentiously reported as a warning about violence to both sides of the campaign. Here is how one headline presented

Docherty's intervention. "Police have warned of disorder and possible violence in the days ahead of the Scottish independence referendum, following a shock poll which put Alex Salmond within touching distance of victory".[29] This was almost the reverse of what Docherty had meant. And much of the press coverage was similar. Indeed, the SPF continued to be concerned about the intemperate language and produced another warning on the eve of poll on the 17th September:

> Any neutral observer could be led to believe Scotland is on the verge of societal disintegration yet nothing could be further from the truth. At this time it is more important than ever that individuals be they politicians, journalists or whoever should carefully consider their words, maintain level heads and act with respect. Respect is not demonstrated by suggesting a minority of mindless idiots are representative of anything. [30]

There was widespread coverage of the call from the Scottish Regional Organiser of the National Union of Journalists, Paul Holleran, for an end to what he called the "intimidation and threats to journalists". This was assumed to refer to the demonstrations at Pacific Quay against BBC bias, and it is true that the NUJ did not accept that BBC journalists there should be subject to calls for their sacking (in fact there was an industrial dispute in BBC Scotland that nearly disrupted the referendum night broadcast). However, what was not widely reported was that the NUJ journalists cited by Holleran who had been the subject of threats reported to the police were in fact Yes supporters. On September 15th he tweeted:

> Just for clarification – the journalists considering police action – not from BBC. Physical violence threats were against two pro-Yes members.

Again, the story was adapted to fit the narrative of nationalist thuggery. For example, the headline on *The Guardian*'s report on the NUJ story read: National Union of Journalists condemns Yes camp's intimidation (15/9/14). Holleran believes his intervention was misreported. He says that there has been widespread concern among journalists in Scotland at the behaviour of the press and is urging the NUJ to hold an inquiry into media coverage of the referendum, including broadcasting, to see what lessons can be learned.

Some of the claims made by the UK press were not just alarmist but positively malign. The *Sunday Express* ran a front page story "UK split to set back cure for cancer" (8/6/14). This was based on a forecast from a consultant that medical research would be damaged if the Union broke up. The claim was rubbished before the day was out by Cancer Research UK who said there was no necessary impact on medical research funding, but this did not reach the front pages. Nor did the rebuttal from Great Ormond Street Hospital to claims that sick Scottish children be excluded from treatment in the London hospital after independence. In the final fortnight of the campaign the press coverage verged on the hysterical. Scottish independence

> "would harm world's poorest" (*The Scotsman* 24/4/14); "Yes vote risks EU veto and Wonga style interest rates" (*Daily Express* 3/9/14); "Criminal gangs could exploit new border to evade arrest" (*Independent* 12/9/14); "700,000 to Leave if Union is Broken" (*International Business Times* 28/7/14)

Days before the poll, the *Sunday Telegraph* ran what is arguably the most tasteless front page of the entire referendum campaign. Four days before the vote it placed a picture of a dead soldier in a coffin under banner headlines reading: 'Scottish soldiers lost their lives defending the UK, what will their relatives say now'. Actually, a number of Scottish veterans had plenty to say and 20 of them, including 102-year-old Desert Rat Jimmy Sinclair, signed a letter condemning this report, and the former chief of staff Lord Dannatt who was quoted in it. But the *Telegraph*'s dead squaddie was preceded by what was surely the most over-the-top front page of the entire campaign.

On the Saturday before polling day, the *Daily Record* ran a front page headline saying that a vote for independence could "trigger a new Great Depression" (12/9/14). The notion that Scotland, a country of five million people, could cause a stock market crash, a global financial crisis and mass unemployment by voting for self-government, was so ridiculous it beggars belief that anyone could seriously have proposed it. There was a source: an official in Deutsche Bank. But all that proved is that there are some very stupid bankers, as the financial crash also demonstrated. Newspapers have a responsibility not only to their readers but also to the quality of public debate.

Some commentators and politicians in the Yes campaign said that the Unionist groupthink in the press didn't matter because people are turning in large numbers to the internet. However, the press still carries clout. Research carried out by YouGov for News UK found that 60 per cent of Scots relied on newspapers and their websites for the majority of their information on the independence debate. This compared to 54 per cent who said they obtained their information from social media and 44 per cent, from the Yes or No camps directly. The most popular source of information was television and radio with 71 per cent.[31] Since television and radio often take their cue from what is in the press, it is clear that newspapers are still a key element in the democratic process. If they are distorted, then democracy is distorted.

The press coverage of the 2014 independence referendum raises fundamental questions about the viability of the democratic process in a media environment where there is an absence of press diversity. A press cannot be said to be free when it all supports the same political line. This is a problem I explore in *Democracy in the Dark* (Saltire) in which I describe the Unionist "group-think" that was evident in the press around the time of the Chancellor George Osborne's Declaration on the Pound. Scotland's misfortune is to be a county with a distinct national political culture but no national media. Most of the press in Scotland is foreign-owned, and while that doesn't necessarily mean they are unable to be objective, in Scotland's case most of them are instinctively, indeed militantly Unionist. This is something that other small countries have faced, such as Norway. In the 1960s, when newspaper closures threatened diversity, it introduced a system of press subsidies to ensure that voters were exposed to a variety of opinions and perspectives, not just at election time but throughout the year. They took this difficult and controversial step because Norway has a constitutional guarantee, not only of press freedom but also diversity of opinion. Other small countries like Denmark have taken similar measures. Democracy doesn't work when voters are not exposed to both sides of the story.

This one-sided and intemperate coverage damaged the credibility of the press almost as much as it damaged the Yes campaign. In the previous chapter I indicated how the press failed to detect until the very last moment the shift of Scottish opinion to independence. The newspapers failed to appreciate the extent to which even a majority of No voters had rejected George Osborne's threat to stop Scots using the pound. Since nearly half of the adult population of Scotland were rethinking their attachment to the Union, it seems remarkable that the press, with all its journalists, did not detect this earlier than it did. This development was noticed on the web, however. Elizabeth Linder, Facebook's politics and government specialist, noted long before the press realised that "Numbers coming out of Scotland are showing that this has the potential to be an extremely close vote... These experiences, of friends influencing friends, matter."

It seems clear that the newspapers allowed their editorial agendas to get in the way of their communication with their readers. And this has had very serious consequences. There is now a very large body of people in Scotland who are deeply disillusioned with the press, to such an extent that they simply no longer believe what is written there. Look at any of the internet sites related to the Yes campaign – We Are The 45%, Hope over Fear, Yes Alliance – and you will now find, not just criticism of mainstream media but a complete rejection of it, as if it were the propaganda arm of a foreign power. For example, Alastair McIntosh, a professional journalist and Quaker, who has written for *The Guardian* and many other publications, says Scotland "requires a free media. One that is rooted in the Scottish people, in our democratic intellect – democratically accountable – and not subaltern to the forces of our internal and inner colonisation where money and fear trump justice and hope".[32] This degree of alienation from the press, shared by hundreds of thousands of Scottish voters, is unprecedented and should be causing alarm, not just in editorial offices, but in the political parties which are also losing their ability to communicate.

The alienated are finding their own ways of exchanging political intelligence through Facebook, Twitter, and blogs. They are looking to websites like *Wings Over Scotland, Newsnet Scotland,*

Bella Caledonia, National Collective and a host of other aggregators and websites for their news. Now, as a newspaper journalist I find this on the one hand inspiring but on the other deeply disturbing. The trouble with social media is that it tends to be an echo chamber, reflecting the views of the committed back to the committed. The newspapers – like them or loathe them – remain important institutions of civil society which have journalistic resources and professional standards of objectivity and accuracy, though I have some difficulty persuading myself that these qualities were much in evidence during the referendum. This lack of balance in the conventional press has created a journalism of grievance based on the internet which has compounded the problem by aping some of the worst characteristics of the mainstream media. There is little attempt to balance comment with factual reportage. At its best the internet material is very good, and some of the best political writing in Scotland is now to be found on websites like *Bella Caledonia* from journalists like James Maxwell. But at its worst, it is poorly researched, self indulgent, opinionated drivel. There is too much of the fanzine about some of the new internet ventures and a lack of editorial discretion and balance.

It seems that, finally, people really are fulfilling the mission of the original digital evangelists and taking the media into their own hands in Scotland, much to the alarm of the conventional press. However, social media can be a platform for abuse, bullying, misinformation, malicious propaganda and political narcissism. There has been a lack of restraint and objectivity and a casual use of extreme language. Some frankly appalling things have been said, for example urging older No voters to "hurry up and die". Suggesting the BBC should be boycotted and everyone who appears on it denounced as a "scab", is hugely counterproductive, as is the denigration of Labour supporters as "Red Tory scum". The task for the independence movement, if it is to succeed, must be to move beyond its own core constituency and address the anxieties of the middle-class, female and elderly voters who rejected independence. Dismissing them as naïve fools too old or dumb to understand is not going to win them to the cause. There is a tendency in the alternative media to narrowness and sectionalism which needs to be curbed.

Newspaper editors scoff at what these organs provide and believe they cannot be matched by random individuals pontificating onto their laptops. However, I think the editors may soon be in for a shock, because this is no longer a matter of socially challenged and isolated loners ejaculating onto Twitter. Many of the new media organisations are upping their game dramatically having discovered, not only that they now have audiences of hundreds of thousands, but that through crowd sourcing via websites like *Indiegogo* and *Kickstarter*, they can also raise hundreds of thousands in hard cash from them. The *Wings Over Scotland* blog run by the former computer games journalist Rev. Stuart Campbell, based in Bath, raised over £50,000 in eight hours in its February 2014 annual fund-raiser, and went on to raise £110,000 over the next two months. For a one-man-band, that's a lot of cash, and it allowed Campbell to publish and distribute a quarter of a million copies of his *Wee Blue Book* promoting Yes arguments.

Rev. Stu is often dismissed as a cybernat, and has been accused – wrongly – of being aggressively homophobic by members of the Yes Campaign. He can be irascible and his tweets are sometimes verging on abuse; but he is another highly intelligent internet entrepreneur who made a very big impression during the referendum campaign and shows no sign of disappearing. In a country where hundreds of thousands of people have simply given up on the conventional press and media, these notably partisan and aggressive websites are becoming highly influential in shaping public opinion.

The new media are not going away just because the referendum result was No. Common Weal has recently hired four journalists to run an alternative news agency. The editor of Bella Caledonia, Mike Small announced a hiring fair in which he has brought in professional broadcasters like ex-BBC presenter Lesley Riddoch, environmental journalist Alastair McIntosh, and Mairi McFadden, one of the key figures behind the culture and arts organisation, National Collective. *Bella Caledonia* also claims to have people covering arts, ecology, social justice and international politics. However, it's not entirely clear how many of them will actually be paid. Other organisations, like Bateman Broadcasting, run by the former BBC presenter, Derek Bateman, have been challenging the broadcasters' monopoly of TV and Radio, and are also branching out into print. There has been an explosion of initiatives on the internet which has altered the media landscape of Scotland forever.

BASHING THE BBC

Not only have many Scots started to question the reliability of newspapers, many have begun to lose confidence in the BBC. Throughout my tours of Scotland I found remarkable numbers of people, even middle-class and middle aged attendees at literary festivals, who were angry at the coverage of the referendum by the BBC. There were two unprecedented demonstrations outside the BBC's headquarters in Pacific Quay during the referendum campaign. These were not organised by Yes Scotland, whose chair, Blair Jenkins, a former BBC man, insists he sees no "structural bias" in BBC reporting. But Tony Blair's former press spokesman, Alistair Campbell, didn't see the difference. On Sunday 14th September he tweeted:

> Had my run ins with BBC, but organised protests like the one going on now is beyond Tebbit, and not far off Putin. Vote YES for intimidation.

There was a certain irony in this, coming from the man who had attacked the BBC and had its Director General sacked for a *Today* report claiming – quite accurately – that his dossiers on Iraq had been "sexed up". But nor was it justified. The demonstrations were not inspired by Alex Salmond as suggested, even though the First Minister did criticise the "unconscious bias" of the BBC. These were not attempts to occupy or incite violence. Public demonstrations are part of the democratic process and do not constitute a threat to press freedom provided they are peaceful, and these were – though very noisy. It is, as a general rule, wrong for politicians to try to put pressure on broadcasters. However, broadcasters are not above legitimate criticism.

The principle object of nationalist fury was the now infamous *Six O'Clock News* broadcast by the BBC's political editor, Nick Robinson, on 11th September. It was an account of an Alex Salmond press conference for international journalists and Robinson said that his question "why should people believe you, a politician, and not the CEOs of large companies" was not answered by Salmond. Unfortunately for him, fully 100,000 had already seen the First Minister's seven-minute answer because it had already gone viral on the internet, and it went on to record half a million views. Robinson may not have liked Salmond's answer – journalists rarely are satisfied by politician's answers – but he should have run some of it in his report. This is a new problem for metropolitan journalists working in a political environment in which new media is beginning to take over from the old. They have to expect that, sometimes, they are going to be held to account in unexpected ways.

On the whole, Robinson's reports were sound, if from a very Westminster point of view. The problem faced by the BBC and the rest of the London-based media was largely one of context. After the YouGov poll on 10th September showing for the first time that Yes was ahead, they descended upon Scotland as if it were already a foreign country. They went on to re-report a whole series of stories that had already been given a good airing in Scotland – such as the claims by Standard Life and RBS that they were making contingency plans to take their headquarters south. I did countless interviews during the final week of the campaign for BBC, ITV, SKY, CNN etc. in which I was repeatedly informed by presenters that 12,000 RBS jobs were going south. "Did I not think that was a major concern"? I pointed out that what most Scots viewers already knew, that the CEO of RBS Ross McEwen had informed staff that there were no job losses involved. I also pointed out that Standard Life had said much the same in the 1990s.

I found myself on numerous UK-based programmes being told how the campaign had been brutal, violent, aggressive and that nationalist thugs had been intimidating journalists and Labour politicians. I tried to explain that, compared with nationalist movements in the Basque region of Spain, Ukraine, or Northern Ireland, this one was strikingly non-violent. But so ingrained was the "story" that Yes equals Nasty Party that it was almost impossible to get a hearing. Sometimes logistics played a part. On one occasion, I was on the Sky News newspaper review with Iain Martin of *The Telegraph* and Kevin McGuire of *The Mirror* – both are notoriously hostile to independence. They were with the presenter in the studio in London; I was in the cold outside Holyrood, and they sniggered in disbelief at my portrayal.

The further problem for the broadcast media – most notably the BBC – is that, having no editorial opinions of their own, they tend to take their lead from the newspapers. Whatever happens to be on their front pages is seen as a guide to the questions to ask, the approach to take, the issues to explore. This is perhaps acceptable during normal elections, but in a referendum like Scotland's where all the press are taking the same political line, this puts the BBC in an invidious position – especially in its news reviews. It has to recount what the main organs of opinion and news are saying, and if they all say that independence will lead to job losses and economic distress, even a Great Depression, then they are bound to ask Yes supporters: "have you taken leave of your senses in asking people to vote for economic apocalypse"? As *The Herald* blogger Jock Morrison put it: "The BBC's "impartiality" generally consisted of giving the Yes side the opportunity to respond to scare stories circulated by supporters of the Union". (23/9/14)

The spillover effect was analysed by Professor John Robertson of the University of the West of Scotland. In January 2014 in a report entitled 'Fairness in the First Year' he concluded that the BBC and STV in Scotland were favouring the No campaign in their news output by a ratio of 3 to 2. The team did a content analysis of 730 hours of BBC Scotland and STV news programmes and the verdict was that negative stories about independence dominated the output of the two Scottish domestic TV channels.

> Both feature a preponderance of anti-independence statements, a majority of anti-independence evidence and a heavy personalisation of the debate around the character of Alex Salmond, with the latter often portrayed as selfish and undemocratic.[33]

The report indicated a predominance of reports leading from the negative, as in: "Questions mount over independence", "6,500 Trident defence jobs under threat", "Electricity costs could rise under independence". The SNP or Yes spokesperson is generally given a right of reply, but the defensive nature of the response itself conveys a message. This report has been criticised, not least by BBC Scotland itself, who complained to the Principal of University of West of Scotland about it. They deny that their coverage is biased, indicating that they gave equal time to both sides. However, I don't believe this, or Robertson's follow-up studies can be ignored.

My opinion, as a viewer, was that BBC Scotland journalists like Glen Campbell, Brian Taylor, and James Cook (the BBC

Scottish correspondent) took their responsibility to be impartial very seriously indeed. They are excellent journalists and in my view wholly unbiased. The same goes for John MacKay and Bernard Ponsonby of STV. The problem is two-fold. They were faced with a press that was hostile to independence and could hardly ignore this. Secondly, when some of the Westminster and UK correspondents trekked north somewhat uncomprehendingly, they did much to damage the BBC's credibility. This certainly happened with the coverage of the RBS story, were the BBC failed to make clear that job losses were not likely on the scale suggested by politicians.

The UK political correspondents were also clearly taking a great deal of the spin from the UK Treasury and Number Ten over stories like RBS and food prices. This was noted later by Robert Peston, the BBC's economics editor on 12 September when he pointed out that the UK Treasury had leaked the story about RBS relocation before the board meeting had actually agreed to publicise it. "There was someone in Number Ten trying to get the banks to co-ordinate on this", a senior banker told Peston. [34] Also, he and *The Guardian* pointed out that supermarket bosses had been rounded up by Number Ten and urged to talk up the risk of food price hikes after independence. [35] There was no indication of this government involvement in the stories when they were originally published.

There was a further problem with the BBC coverage: a tendency to report the referendum campaign as if it were a conventional election allocating balance across parties. Stuart Cosgrove, Channel 4's director of creative diversity, challenged the BBC publicly on this. "I was watching the rolling BBC News very closely" he told BBC radio, "and it was clear that notions of balance were being predicated on a party political basis. It would go from Cameron to Miliband to Clegg and back. If you took a different premise – it's a yes/no question – then Patrick Harvie of the Greens should have had exactly the same coverage as Ed Miliband". [36] The BBC responded to Cosgrove that their coverage was "accurate and impartial, in line with our editorial guidelines". I am afraid that this was not acceptable and that the BBC lost a great deal of its credibility in Scotland as a result.

Under normal circumstances, political parties are loathe to criticise the BBC because voters trust it more than them. However, there has been a breakdown of trust in Scotland, and the BBC has to address this somehow. The argument that it has made mistakes should not be dismissed. Nor can observations such as this from Paul Mason, the former *Newsnight* Economics Editor, who tweeted on 12th September 2014: "Not since Iraq have I seen BBC News working at propaganda strength like this. So glad I'm out of there." As for the press, I can only repeat that in my view coverage was unjustifiably sympathetic to the Unionist side. And I don't think it was entirely unconscious. I am a hack myself and I know how they work. I believe in their hearts many Scottish and UK journalists knew exactly what they were doing to the Yes campaign. It is called "monstering".

CHAPTER FIVE

The Nationalist Janus – The Two Faced Bastard

One of the most memorable events of the 2014 independence referendum was the BBC's Big Big Debate, which took place in front of 7,500 16 and 17 year-olds at the SSE Hydro in Glasgow one week before the referendum. It probably changed history, if only because the intelligent contributions from the first time voters nailed forever the lie that they are too young to participate in elections. For inexplicable reasons, Better Together elected to put the case for the Union in the hands of the Scottish Tory leader, Ruth Davidson, and the Respect MP, George Galloway. Yes fielded the Deputy First Minister, Nicola Sturgeon and the Scottish Green co-convenor, Patrick Harvie.

It wasn't one of Better Together's finest outings. Galloway, resplendent in one of his famous hats, was booed by the young audience when he alluded to the great war against fascism as an argument against nationalism. In his "Just Say Naw" speaking tour of Scotland, Galloway had claimed that the SNP were fascist fellow travellers during the Second World War. As he put it: "the leaders of the SNP were openly willing a Nazi invasion."[37] This equation of Scottish nationalism and fascism was one of the unavoidable underlying themes in the referendum, especially on the left. "Blood and soil" – a reference to the Nazi slogan "Blut und Boden" – was the shorthand used widely on social media to demonise the Yes campaign, equating independence for Scotland with extreme nationalism.

The Labour blogger Ian Smart, a former president of the Scottish Law Society, said that the SNP was a neo-fascist organisation that "celebrated Nazi sympathisers at their annual conference" and compared Alex Salmond to Mussolini. Euan McColm of *The Scotsman* tweeted about "a little cup of blood and a little cup of soil". Even the chair of Better Together, Alistair Darling, referred to "blood and soil nationalism" in an interview with the *New Statesman* in June 2014. Yes posters, particularly in West Central Scotland, were frequently defaced with swastikas. Yes campaigners claimed that some Unionists had taken to giving them Nazi salutes in the street. The worst example of this was caught on film at the Loyalist victory demonstration in Glasgow's

George Square on the 19th September 2014, when six people were arrested after violent exchanges involving pro-Unionists giving Yes campaigners the stiff arm.

The SNP is not an extremist or neo-fascist organisation and the last time anything like "blood and soil" nationalism showed its head in the party was in the form of the tartan splinter group "Seed of the Gael" in the 1970s. It was quickly expelled. The SNP under Alex Salmond and his predecessors has been a strictly non-violent, democratic parliamentary movement, similar to the civic nationalist movements that grew up, albeit under very different circumstances, in Eastern Europe in the 1990s. Despite Scotland's proximity to Ireland, the SNP has resisted any connection with Irish nationalism, Sinn Fein, or the IRA. It has no ethnic or racial criterion for membership, had the first Muslim MSP in Holyrood, and campaigns for open borders and increased immigration to Scotland. And many prominent nationalists – my mother included – were pacifists. The modern Scottish National Party since it emerged in the 1960s owed more to the nationalism of Gandhi than Gerry Adams.

It is, anyway, wrong to conflate the Yes campaign with the SNP. Many of the most energetic activists in the Yes campaign were from the Green Party and the Scottish Socialists. Others had no party allegiance whatever and became involved through organisations like Women for Independence, Asians for Independence, the Radical Independence Conference, National Collective or the radical think tank Common Weal. The attitude of the Yes campaign was defiantly non-sectarian and any trace of anti-Englishness or romantic Braveheart Scottishness was expunged in short order. There were no celebrations organised by Yes or the SNP in June 2014, on the 700th anniversary of the Battle of Bannockburn, when Robert the Bruce had defeated the English Army. Yes did not authorise the demonstrations against bias at the BBC. The abuse that JK Rowling received after she announced her £1m donation to Better Together in June was condemned by everyone connected with the Yes campaign, and was not organised by SNP "cybernats" or anyone else in the independence movement. They knew that the first thing that would discourage Scots from voting Yes was any suggestion that there would be border posts, that English people would be sent home or that there could be ethnic conflict in Scotland.

So, it was an uphill struggle for the Unionists to tar the Yes campaign with the brush of extremism. Which doesn't mean they didn't give it their best shot. On 7th April 2014, Lord Robertson, the former Labour Defence Secretary and Shadow Scottish Secretary, delivered a speech to the Brookings Institute in Washington in which he said that independence for Scotland would be a "victory for the forces of darkness" and would give "the dictators, the persecutors, the oppressors, the annexers, the aggressors and the adventurers across the planet, the biggest pre-Christmas present of their lives". The former General Secretary of NATO went on to warn that the "Balkanization of Britain" would be "cataclysmic" for Europe and "a tragedy with incalculable consequences". Not one to mince his words, Lord Robertson had often in the past talked of the "dark side of nationalism", and warned that the seeds of extremism lie in Scottish National Party. [38]

The issue raised its head again after an interview that the First Minister Alex Salmond gave in March to Tony Blair's former press secretary, Alistair Campbell, in which Salmond appeared to praise the authoritarian Russian President Vladimir Putin. The interview for *GQ Magazine* had been conducted before the annexation of Crimea, however it was printed contemporaneously with the emerging war over Ukrainian separatism. Given the reputation of his interviewer, Salmond might have been wiser to have chosen his words rather more carefully. What he said when asked what he thought about the Russian Prime Minister was this:

> Well, obviously, I don't approve of a range of Russian actions, but I think Putin's more effective than the press he gets, I would have thought, and you can see why he carries support in Russia.

Pressed on whether he admired the Russian leader, Salmond said:

> Certain aspects. He's restored a substantial part of Russian pride and that must be a good thing. There are aspects of Russian constitutionality and the inter-mesh with business and politics that are obviously difficult to admire. Russians are fantastic people, incidentally, they are lovely people.

This caused a furious parliamentary and media row which lasted for weeks and led to calls for Salmond to apologise and even resign – both of which he refused to do. Numerous attempts were made to equate Salmond with Putin such as in The *Spectator* magazine (16/9/14), which observed that they both liked "being noticed on the international stage and say that being seen to possess a distinctive national identity is more important than some of the difficult consequences [of nationalism]". In fact, it is hard to think of two politicians who are less alike than the rotund, social democratic Alex Salmond and the ex-KGB hard man. But it fitted the narrative of those who believe that there is something intrinsically right wing about nationalism which leads inevitably to dictatorship.

But if Putin doesn't fit, how about Mussolini? Tom Gallagher, an emeritus Professor of Peace Studies at Bradford University, has pursued the "autocratic" Alex Salmond like a dark shadow for years claiming that he has profound authoritarian tendencies. In an article for *Harry's Place* in 2009 he compared him to Benito Mussolini, the Italian fascist who in his early years appeared to be somewhat to the left in his policies. He and the Labour blogger Ian Smart claimed that in power, Salmond would meet insuperable economic difficulties and in Smart's words would blame "the Poles and Pakis" for his failures. There is something of an obsession in Labour circles with tartan fascism and the notion that the Yes campaign must inevitably turn Nazi because of its nationalist politics. In his book, *Fascist Scotland*, the St Andrews University lecturer, Gavin Bowd claimed – with very little real evidence – that "the roots of fascism run deep in Scotland", and that the beast was in heat again. "Today, the ruling party of Scotland has nationalism as its creed and is suspiciously coy about its own history" he wrote. "The Scottish electorate now appears more receptive to radical nationalism than Mosley's blackshirts could ever dream of." This all reached a kind of bizarre and tasteless climax on the anniversary of D-Day in June 2014 when Smart tweeted: "Are we really going to go through the entire D-Day weekend without anybody pointing out the SNP were on the Nazi side?". This was a reference to the former leader of the SNP in the 1960s, Arthur Donaldson.

In fact, Donaldson had nothing to do with fascism or the Nazis. He was a pacifist and was interned in Barlinnie Prison for six weeks during World War II for calling on Scots to refuse the draft. MI5 kept a file on Donaldson which included some lurid fantasies from informants about his being a Scottish Quisling who wanted a Nazi victory. But not even the Labour Secretary of State, Tom Johnston – a fierce opponent of the SNP – believed this and he had Donaldson released from prison. Nationalists like to remind Labour, in turn, that the leader of the British Union of Fascists in the 1930s, Oswald Mosley, had been a Labour MP before he donned the black shirt. As the writer Gerry Hassan observed:

> Imagine the political stramash there would be today in some quarters if Oswald Mosley had been an SNP MP before he decided to become leader of Britain's fascists? For some, it would be the defining fact of the independence debate.

A good point well made.[39]

Political Scottish nationalism is a very recent phenomenon; it only came into existence in 1934 and the Scottish National Party spent most of the next half century rowing with itself in electoral obscurity. At its birth, the SNP certainly had some colourful characters around, including the poet, Hugh MacDiarmid, who was certainly anti-English and listed one of his recreations in *Who's Who* as "Anglophobia." CM Grieve, to use the real name of the journalist from Langholm, was a brilliant modernist poet, though he was ideologically opaque in much of his writings, and appeared to favour Mussolini in the early 1920s. Labour insist that he had Nazi sympathies; MacDiarmid wrote favourably of the Nazi-supporting Wyndham Lewis on the virtues of "Blutesgefuel" in the early 1930s.[40] But the truth is that Grieve, who parted company with the SNP after the War, was a communist, an eventual out-and-out Stalinist, who approved of the suppression of the Hungarian uprising in 1956. The clue is in his poetry – he was author of three 'Hymns to Lenin'.

Among the other colourful characters who were attracted to the Scottish National Party at its birth was Harrow-educated Robert Bontine Cunninghame Graham, a landowner, poet, historian, rancher and former gaucho in Argentina. Cunninghame Graham helped to found the National Party in 1928 and became the first president of the SNP in 1934. He was similarly ideologically promiscuous. Don Roberto, as he was affectionately known, had also been the co-founder of the Scottish Labour Party with Keir

Hardie at the end of the 19th Century. He also attended the Marxist Congress of the Second International in Paris with Hardie and Eleanor Marx in 1889, and before that had been a Liberal MP. The SNP has therefore always been able to say, with some justification, that socialism is as much a part of its DNA, as it is in Labour's, though this has never stopped Labour calling the SNP the Tartan Tories.

So, the fascist slur is just that. Nevertheless, the nationalist connection has often presented serious ideological and even organisational issues for the Scottish National Party. It has sometimes found itself resisting overtures from extremist organisations in Europe like Umberto Bossi's Lombard League, the Belgian Vlaams Belang, or the militant Basques ETA. Most nationalist parties in Europe, like Marine Le Pen's National Front, are cultural or ethnic nationalists, opposed to immigration and the European Union. The SNP stands for precisely the reverse of these policies, but guilt by association is a perennial problem for civic nationalists. The SNP is also sometimes compared to the United Kingdom Independence Party as a 'natural' party of the right – "two peas in the same hard pod" according to *The Times* columnist David Aaronovitch. And of course, opponents of Scottish nationalism used to chant: "SNP, BNP – there's only one letter between them". The drumbeat of "blood and soil" is one reason why the SNP and the Yes campaign had such difficulty with the Scottish press in the referendum. Newspapers, especially those London-based, rarely hesitated to recycle offensive or anti-English tweets and internet postings as evidence of thuggish extremism by supporters of independence. These had nothing to do with the Yes campaign, however, and there were far more abusive and vicious and racist things being tweeted from south of the border about Scotland, as we saw in the previous chapter. Death threats to Alex Salmond and his deputy Nicola Sturgeon somehow got lost in the hysteria about racist "cybernats". Labour MP Jim Murphy exploited this presumption of thuggishness to the full during his 100 cities soap-box tour, where he spliced together camera phone footage of nationalist hecklers and said they were an organised gang sent by the Yes Scotland campaign to intimidate him. There is simply an expectation, almost an unspoken assumption in many parts of the media, that the SNP and the independence movement must, in some way, be of the far right because it based its appeal on nation rather than class.

Hostility to nationalism as a political philosophy runs very deep in Britain, at least on the left. This is largely because of the extreme right-wing nationalist movements that ravaged European democracies in the first half of the last century and led to the Second World War, the Holocaust, the persecution of homosexuals and other minorities. In parallel, there was a reaction amongst British intellectuals to the Little Englander jingoism of the First World War. The war poets, and writers like George Orwell, did much to undermine the values of old-style British nationalism. Poems like Wilfred Owen's 'Dulce Et Decorum Est' are a standard text in schools, and expose nationalism and patriotism as handmaidens of militarism.

Among UK liberals most thinking on nationalism largely begins and ends with George Orwell and his essay, 'Notes on Nationalism' in 1945.[41] In it, Orwell defines nationalism as: "identifying oneself with a single nation or other unit, placing it beyond good and evil and recognising no other duty than that of advancing its interests." Nationalism is, he says, "inseparable from the desire for power". Orwell writes almost as if it were a psychiatric illness. He says its adherents not only lose a sense of right and wrong, but become incapable of understanding arguments or accepting facts that don't fit with their preconceptions. Nationalists will, he says, 'generally claim superiority not only in military power and political virtue, but in art, literature, sport, structure of the language, the physical beauty of the inhabitants, and perhaps even in climate, scenery and cooking.' Well, perhaps not in Scotland, what with the weather, and the food.

Speaking directly of Irish and Scottish nationalism, Orwell observed: "The Celt is supposed to be spiritually superior to the Saxon – simpler, more creative, less vulgar, less snobbish, etc. – but the usual power hunger is there under the surface". This essay was plainly a work of propaganda, still fighting the war against fascism, and made no attempt to understand the origins of political nationalism and democracy in Europe. It has been extraordinarily influential, however, and has been cited by almost every critic of the Scottish independence at some time or other as conclusive proof of the inherent evil of any politics based on nation.

Orwell's portrayal of nationalism as a one-way ticket to extremism and violent obscurantism resurfaced during the referendum campaign, even among writers who accept that Alex Salmond is no Adolf Hitler. The liberal columnist Will Hutton said in *The Observer* ten days before the referendum that "If Britain can't find a way of sticking together, it is the death of the liberal enlightenment before the atavistic forces of nationalism and ethnicity – a dark omen for the 21st century". David Aaronovitch of The Times argued during the referendum campaign that the process of "othering", of creating divisions on the basis of national identity, was a process not dissimilar to that which Orwell described. He and other Unionists argued that the virulence of the cybernats, their extreme reaction to criticism, and the violent language of Jim Murphy's street hecklers, showed that nationalism hasn't changed its obsessional spots. Aaronovitch and others also accused those who argued that Scotland had developed a different political culture of nationalist myth-making. In fact, he pointed out on Twitter, Scots are just as likely to hold anti-immigration or xenophobic views as English people. "There is nothing about the Scots that makes them better people". And of that, he is right: Scots are no more immune to prejudice than anyone else.

My response to this charge was – is – that this is a question of politics and history, not race or culture. The Scots are not superior in any way to English people, and the case for Scottish self-determination has nothing to do with "othering" another social group or nationality. Though, if it is "othering" to oppose right-wing conservatism, then Scots plead guilty. It is simply a fact, a legacy of history, that Scotland is dominated by two parties of the social democratic left: Labour and the SNP. Their programmes are almost identical in broad ideology, though the SNP has been much further left in policy terms in recent years than Labour, which is the main reason it won a landslide victory in the 2011 Scottish parliamentary elections. What motivates Scottish voters is not "Scottish exceptionalism" as Labour call it, but issues like university tuition fees, the abolition of prescription charges, the rejection of private provision in the Scottish NHS, free personal care for the elderly and many other policies usually described as "progressive universalism". Labour claim that these left wing policies – which they call the "free stuff" or the "something for nothing" society – have been adopted by the SNP, not from a true commitment to social democracy, but out of opportunism. They are merely the means by which Alex Salmond has sought to gain power to promote his nationalist ends and divide the UK on ethnic lines to promote his "Scottish parliamentary dictatorship", as the Labour MP Anas Sarwar described it in the House of Commons in January 2013.

There is a frustrated sense of entitlement underlying Labour's critique of Scottish nationalism. Labour dominated Scottish politics in the 1980s and 90s and they believe that Scotland is their natural territory. The Scottish nationalists must therefore have used devious tactics to seize it from them by manufacturing grievance against England and imposing their "politics of identity". In fact, the SNP rarely deploy identity in their message, and Nicola Sturgeon, the new leader of the party, has made her commitment to social democracy paramount. It is, anyway, offensive to the Scottish voters to suggest that they can't tell the difference between a social democrat and a dictator. One of the most sophisticated electorates in the world is not so stupid that it can be bribed by a nationalist demagogue. The Scots were not hypnotised by identity politics, but turned against Labour because of the Iraq war, Trident and Tony Blair's promotion of market reforms to public services like the NHS. The claim that the SNP has merely borrowed Labour policies begs the question of why Labour abandoned them in the first place. The party's problem in Scotland, as its former leader, Johann Lamont, made clear in her resignation statement in October 2014, is that the UK Labour leadership has treated the Scottish Labour Party as a "branch office" and prevented it responding to the social democratic inclinations of Scottish voters.

These taunts about the extreme right are essentially playground politics and obscure the real issue: which is that nationalism appears to be replacing class as the leading edge of progressive politics in Scotland. The referendum was a transformative event, and, for good or ill, Scottish nationalism is now a mass movement as never before. 1.6 million people voted for Scotland to be independent, defying their traditional party, Labour, the UK state, the opposition parties and most of the press and media. Scots even defied Barack Obama, Hillary Clinton, and the Pope, who all urged Scots to be wary of secession. There has never been an independence movement like this in Scotland before – and it isn't going to go away. One of the most pressing questions in British politics, therefore, is what happens to this nationalism now that it has been frustrated in its objective of departing from the UK.

Though I voted Yes in the referendum, I do not regard myself as a nationalist of any description and have never been tempted to join the Scottish National Party, even though I am usually described as one of their leading "cheer-leaders". My support for what the SNP has done in Scotland is almost entirely because of their social democratic policies and their commitment to social justice, nuclear disarmament, racial integration, open borders, increased immigration and the defence of public services. I believe their adoption of these essentially socialist values is sincere, even though Alex Salmond has, from time to time, appeared to be open to influence from neoliberal economics. In 2008, in an interview with Iain Dale, Salmond appeared to support Margaret Thatcher's economic policies: "We [the Scots] didn't mind the economic side so much. We didn't like the social side at all." Before the 2008 crash the First Minister became far too close to the Scottish banks, RBS and HBOS, and almost became a press spokesmen for them. He justifies this now by pointing out that it was his job to support financial services which employ over 100,000 Scots and account for 6% of GDP.

I had no qualms about voting Yes in the independence referendum because I believe that Scotland (and rUK) would be a better society if it ran its own affairs. But I've personally never really "got" nationalism, patriotism and love of country, much as I never "got" religion. I grew up in an atheist household and find religious observance and doctrine incomprehensible. Similarly, I can understand why people get emotional at football matches, and succumb to love of place, but I've never really felt it myself. For example, I cringed when I read the first line of Gordon Brown's book *My Scotland, Our Britain*: "Some people have a love-hate relationship with their country. Mine is a love-love relationship". Of course, some people say that this is patriotism (the last refuge of the scoundrel) rather than nationalism. But the two cannot really be separated.

If I am honest, I still retain some of the latent hostility to nationalism that I had in my leftist youth. After all, didn't Karl Marx reject nationalism as reactionary, as an essentially "bourgeois phenomenon". "The working-class have no country", he said in *The Communist Manifesto*. Ever since then, nationalism has been regarded by the left as a means of dividing the working-class and diverting them from the true goal of socialism. This remained the dominant view on the left until very recently and was most famously articulated by the Labour MP Brian Wilson in his great debates with the SNP in the 1970s. And it is undeniable that nationalism was, and is, used by the ruling classes as an antidote to socialism.

The Labour Party founder, Keir Hardie, was dismayed in 1914 when the workers of Britain and Germany, who had been the most receptive to the ideals of socialism, went in their millions to the trenches to fight each other in the cause of their respective nations. Nationalist movements were only given qualified support by the left in the last century when they involved struggles against imperialism in African countries, or in South Africa against apartheid. But this was only seen as progressive to the extent that it undermined capitalist imperialism. And it didn't apply to Scotland, except in the writings of the neo-nationalist, Tom Nairn, in *The Break-Up of Britain* in 1977.

All this sounds like rather quaint ideological archaeology today, now that Marxism has apparently been swept into the "dustbin of history" along with the Berlin Wall and the Soviet Union. But the Marxist view of nationalism still influences attitudes to Scottish nationalism today, and not just on the old left. The arguments were redeployed by Ed Miliband, the Labour leader, and Gordon Brown, in the referendum campaign, when they argued that by splitting off from the UK state, the Scots would be "abandoning" the poor working people of England. Brown said that it was Scotland's moral duty to remain in the Union to ensure that there was "pooling and sharing" of resources for the benefit of all the citizens of the UK. This is very much the language of socialist internationalism recast in a post-Marxist era. George Galloway said that it was "immoral" for Scotland to seek to be "richer" at the expense of others in the UK "who would be made poorer as a result". These arguments certainly held sway in the 1970s and 80s when Scots rejected the crass materialism of the SNP's "It's Scotland's Oil" campaign.

But during the referendum campaign, when large numbers of people entered the political process for the first time, it became clear to anyone prepared to look that this was popular mobilisation of young people and working-class people in Scotland in a way that Marxism never achieved – at least not since the days of John MacLean in the 1920s, who was also, of course, a Scottish nationalist. Marxists always accused nationalists of inviting people to support a reactionary abstraction, the nation, that didn't really exist, except in folk tale and legend. But for the thousands of people involved in the Yes campaign, their better nation seemed a lot more concrete and rational, as well as inspirational, than the dry abstraction of proletarian internationalism. After all, what is the international working-class? Has it ever really existed outside of Trotskyist theory?

Clearly, thousands of people were inspired by the ideal of a more just society in Scotland, and it is surely unjust to criticise them for that, or accuse them of being racist or infected with a psychological disease. Those tens of thousands who registered to vote for the first time, consumed the literature and took part in debates, were not nationalist zealots motivated by hatred. They were not the creatures of Orwellian demonology, fired by a mystic vision of ethnic superiority in everything from religion to baking. The independence campaign mobilised people in a way class politics no longer can and, in Britain, never has. And the mobilisation was inseparable from its manifestly progressive ideals. After the 2014 referendum, the left has to ask itself whether it makes sense any longer to regard nationalism as an inherently reactionary and undemocratic force.

It wasn't always so, of course. Historically, nationalism and democracy went hand-in-hand. The revolutions of 1848, which gave rise to *The Communist Manifesto*, were not socialist in any obvious sense of the word, but were democratic and nationalist. This is why 1848 used to be called the "Springtime of Nations". In *The Rights of Man*, Tom Paine took it to be self evident, not only that people have a right to liberty, but that they live in "natural communities" – in nations defined by geography, culture and history. Theorists of nationalism like Ernest Gellner in *Nations and Nationalism* and *Conditions of Liberty* follow Paine in accepting that, whatever we think of nationalism, democracy as we understand it is inconceivable without it and both were, according to Gellner, products of industrialisation. A precondition of democracy was the creation of a viable state with a monopoly of violence in a defined geographical area with a common culture. During the industrial revolution, these states became the focus of democratic struggles, first against foreign oppression, and then against internal oppression by the governing elite. Modern democracy arose out of this struggle by the people to govern themselves, but always within this defined geographical and cultural space: the nation.

The debate in Scotland has not really been between nationalism and internationalism, as is often suggested by many Unionists, but between two competing nationalisms: British and Scottish. Both England and Scotland are ancient cultures, dating back to the middle ages, and they have spent much of that time in conflict with each other. The Union of 1707 achieved a settlement – supposedly a constitutional contract – by which the two nations would occupy the same political and economic space. This was a great achievement, even though it was of course pre-democratic. The Scottish Parliament that voted for its own extinction in 1707 was not elected by the people of Scotland but was more like a chamber of commerce representing the burgesses, lairds, and lords. However, the Union was a remarkable exercise in enlightenment statesmanship and endured right through into the democratic era.

As I argued in my book *Road to Referendum*, political nationalism is a novel concept for most Scots precisely because the Union was so successful for so long. Scotland is not like Ireland. There, political agitation against the Union began almost as soon as it joined in 1801, became progressively more militant over the next century, and culminated in civil war. Throughout this period, Scots were enthusiastic partners in the Union and the British Empire and there was no significant nationalist party seeking repudiation of the Union until 1934. Even then, Scottish nationalism was a feeble political force, really, until the 1990s. The history of Scotland over the last forty years has been a case, if you like, of unintended nationalism. Scots were quite content with the United Kingdom as it emerged from the Second World War – with the welfare state, nationalised industries, regional policy, the NHS and social security. But as these values have been eroded, first by Margaret Thatcher and then by Tony Blair (at least in Scottish eyes), the Scots found themselves turning to nationalism the better to defend the achievements of social democracy.

All this conforms to Gellner's definition of "civic nationalism" as a movement which arises in specific circumstances to address a perceived democratic deficit. Scottish nationalism has also, paradoxically, proved itself to be the most dynamic vehicle for progressive change in the UK. The social democratic policies pursued by the Scottish Parliament since its restoration in 1999 became, as Alex Salmond argued in his Hugo Young lecture to *The Guardian* in 2011, a beacon of progressive politics for the rest of the UK, even if the rest of the UK isn't particularly in the market for beacons right now. The point is that the Scots have been demanding greater democratic control of their affairs, not in order to prove their exceptionalism in an Orwellian sense, but in order to pursue this different philosophy of social organisation. In their attitudes to war, nuclear weapons and Europe, the nationalists are more internationalist than the Unionists.

It seems to me that self-determination for Scotland is the only sensible solution to this contradiction between Scottish aspirations and UK political reality, and if that's what nationalism means, so be it. Scotland already feels, in many ways, like one of those small Northern European countries, like Denmark, Norway or Finland. Countries where wealth differentials are relatively low, social security is high, public services are valued and the state is seen as, on the whole, a beneficial partner in the economy. The UK, meanwhile, is moving in a very different direction. Decades of low taxation have led to great inequalities of wealth, made concrete in inner London property values. The state is increasingly being seen as a bureaucratic intrusion by many people and public services like the NHS are being subjected, if not to outright privatisation, then to increasing market-based reforms, in England at least.

What is the point of trying to force Scotland and England to remain in an incorporating Union while they pursue these different paths? Perhaps, as I have argued, if the UK adopted the divided sovereignty concept of federalism, the contradiction might be resolved, at least for a time. But without a fundamental constitutional transformation it is very difficult to see how this United Kingdom is supposed to hold together. The infamous Barnett Formula – the method of calculating increases in Scottish public spending – is going to become the central focus of this regional divergence, as the UK uses fiscal restraint to rein in the ambitions of the Scottish parliament. Meanwhile, the move toward English Votes for English Laws – the principle of which is now accepted by both Labour and Conservatives – will reduce significantly the presence of Scottish MPs in Westminster. The dynamic is a federal one, but in the absence of any sincere move towards creating a federal state, Scotland continues to face a hard choice of whether to remain in the UK or become independent.

As I argued in Chapter Two, in the attempt to suppress

nationalism in Scotland, the UK state took what was, in my view, an unwise step by telling Scots that if they voted Yes to independence then they would lose the pound – the economic expression of the Union. Suddenly, the Union appeared no longer as a joint project, but as rUK property. This introduced a coercive element into the relationship between Scotland and England that was disturbing to many Scots. Suddenly, Scotland was no longer a partner nation but a subordinate region. Indeed, my own view is that the Union, as Scots understand it, died when Tory Chancellor George Osborne told Scots that he would build a financial Hadrian's Wall to stop Scots using their own currency.

BUTTERFLY REBELLION

So, civic nationalism has been the only way for Scotland to express its continued commitment to social democratic values. This is all very well and very much the gospel according to Gellner. Scottish nationalism as represented in the 2014 referendum was not an ethnic nationalism based on racial or cultural exclusiveness.

However, this doesn't entirely resolve the broader problem with nationalism which, for all its progressive variants is still, at root, a politics based not on social values and universalism, but on nationhood and, ultimately, ethnicity in its broadest sense. There is always a fear, sometimes expressed in the corners of the Yes campaign, that some of the powerful forces unleashed by the referendum could go in an extremist direction. Some of the language of the defeated forces of independence has been fierce, claiming that Scotland has been cheated out of independence by lies, media distortion deceit and even a rigged referendum.

Some 94,000 people have signed a petition calling for a "revote" on the grounds that the referendum was manipulated. The nationalist *Butterfly Rebellion* website claimed that the referendum had been rigged because No supporters were celebrating almost before the polls closed. (In fact, this was probably because Peter Kellner of YouGov announced on the basis of his panel exit poll that he was "99% certain that Better Together had won".) The result left a profound sense of grievance amongst the losers – a belief, as Gordon Wilson put it in his book *Scotland: Battle for Independence*, that the full forces of a "colonial power" (i.e. England) had been deployed against Scotland: the BBC, banks, business. Many thousands of Scots who had been politicised during the campaign, and had believed their own propaganda, simply could not believe that they had lost.

Could this sense of grievance turn into a violent form of nationalism? Could the democratic, poetic and peaceful Yes Campaign spawn a militant independence movement? It is always possible. In some ways, it has been surprising that the national movement in Scotland has been so peaceful, given our proximity to Northern Ireland. I do not myself believe that this is going to happen, largely because democratic behaviour is now so much a part of Scots' concept of themselves. This is like the way the Scottish football supporters, the Tartan Army, turned away from fighting and became famous for holding joyous street parties because that really annoyed the English supporters. The independence campaign showed remarkable self-discipline despite being faced with a hostile media. Nevertheless we are dealing with powerful emotions when we talk of the destiny of nations. The task of all parties in the post-referendum period will be to ensure that the very positive forces unleashed by the Yes campaign continue to enliven Scottish democracy and do not congeal into grievance.

THE JANUS FACE

The writer Tom Nairn famously wrote that nationalism invariably presents a Janus face. It can be progressive, emancipatory, even internationalist. But it can also be negative, inward looking, xenophobic and racist. Nairn was – and is – a Scottish nationalist and has probably done more to rehabilitate nationalism than any other writer since Gellner himself. However, his argument is that nationalism in all its forms exhibits this fatal dualism: "All nationalism is both healthy and morbid", he wrote in *The Break-Up of Britain*, "both progress and regress are inscribed in its genetic code from the start."[42] His argument is that nationalism is, on the whole, positive. He claims that modern nationalism, since its birth during the French Revolution, has saved the world from imperial hegemony and domination. It not only destroyed the old European dynasties in the 19th Century and blew away the British Empire in the 20th; civic nationalism also undermined and destroyed Soviet communism as small nations in central Europe asserted their right to self-determination. Like Gellner, his mentor, Nairn sees nationalism as an expression of modernity, not a reaction against it. And of course, being a Scottish nationalist, Nairn sees what has happened in Scotland as a triumphant vindication of all that he has been arguing. For has not Scotland saved us from the tyranny of neoliberalism, the City of London and the Westminster establishment?

But we can never, as Tom Nairn himself argues, regard any nationalism as intrinsically progressive. There is always the other face to consider. We can all agree that in Eastern Europe, the Nordic countries, even in large parts of Latin America, civic nationalism has been a positive and progressive force. However, it is also the case that the nasty side of the Janus has been on the march also. Anti-immigration populism and Islamophobia have also been muscling in on the nationalist scene in Europe and perhaps also in Britain, where anti-European sentiment is driving Conservative politics to the right.

Some contemporary theorists of nationalism see aspects of this nationalist populism as a good thing. One of them is the Dutch writer Jeroen Zandberg, leader of the rather singular organisation the Unrepresented Nations and Peoples Organisation, which represents ethnic groups not organised in the United Nations, such as the Tibetans. In *The Politics of Freedom*, Zandberg rehearses much of the Gellner/Nairn positive case for nationalism, arguing that democracy is impossible without it. However, he goes further and argues that a prime "objective of nationalism is to have all members of the nation identify with the same culture and thereby each other". He is thus an outspoken and unashamed opponent of multiculturalism, which he says is an "apartheid which privileges foreigners". His idea of self-determination is a cultural nationalism which excludes diversity and rigidly controls immigration.

Zandberg claims to be a liberal and a democrat, but I find his form of ethnically exclusive civic nationalism unattractive. Mind you, there are liberals putting similar arguments in the UK, though without the hostility to immigration. The founding editor of *Prospect Magazine*, David Goodhart, wrote a Demos pamphlet called 'Progressive Nationalism' in 2006, arguing that cultural uniformity was essential for social progress. You cannot have a common welfare state unless you have common values. He argued that the left had got it wrong about immigration and that, unchecked, it and multiculturalism can damage social cohesion and make welfare democracy impossible. And he also

112

argues, rightly in my view, that the left have consistently got it wrong about nationalism and internationalism, which are not antinomies. Internationalism is impossible without nation states that have liberal democratic structures.

It is ironic that Goodhart, who is no friend of Alex Salmond, is the leading proponent in England of progressive nationalism. And again, while I am personally uncomfortable with the rejection of multiculturalism, I have to agree with much of what he says. "Nations remain the building blocks of international co-operation and only they can bring democratic legitimacy to global governance", he wrote in *The Guardian*, "But if people are squeamish about the word 'nation' they should use another: citizenship or just society".[43] Some hope that more open-minded advocates of English nationalism will be able to open a dialogue with the on-going Yes campaign. That they will follow the lead made by the singer Billy Bragg who was such a valuable and poetic force in the Scottish referendum campaign. Certainly, progressive nationalism looks like the only game in town right now.

In the 2014 referendum we have seen (and it is still going on) one of the most engaging and inspirational affirmations of civic nationalism in Europe since the fall of the Berlin Wall. Thousands of Scottish voters have been motivated to get involved in politics in the hope that they can, in this small corner of Europe, create a fairer society. I cannot see that this particular variety of social democratic self-determination can possibly be equated with the dark side of Slobodan Milosevic, Mussolini, Jean-Marie Le Pen or any of the other nationalist bogeys of the left. You can never say anything absolute about nationalism, such is its obvious diversity. Nationalism, like democracy itself, takes many and varied forms, is very much a product of history and contains good and bad, sometimes in the same movement. But we just have to make the best of it. As Harold Macmillan said in his "Winds of Change" speech in Cape Town in February 1960:

> One of the constant facts of political life in Europe has been the emergence of independent nations, especially since the end of the War, the processes which gave birth to the nation states of Europe have been repeated all over the world... Whether we like it or not, this growth of national consciousness is a political fact. We must all accept it as a fact.

CHAPTER SIX

The Constitution – The 15% Federal Solution

It is a truth, universally acknowledged, that constitutions are dry and boring. Constitutionalists are horrible, legal, pedantic, nit-picky people who go on about things like indivisible sovereignty, asymmetrical federalism, non-incorporating unions, fiscal autonomy, Treaty of Westphalia, the d'Hondt method. Nationalism, at least in its progressive variety, is exciting, inspirational, poetic, transformative, heroic. It is about creative destruction. Constitutionalists are like the parent who arrives after the party is over and tell the young people to clear up.

But there is a reason why constitutions are boring. This is because in politics, especially nationalist and revolutionary politics, the drama can get way out of hand. People get drunk on rhetoric, intoxicated by principle, dig in, refuse to negotiate and then it all turns nasty. If revolutions, like Saturn, generally end up by eating their children, constitutions offer counselling and a crèche. Law is there to manage conflict and resolve contradictions by the application of reason and reconciliation. But before doing so, I want to explain a glaring contradiction in my own thinking, on which I have been taken to task.

In my book *Road to Referendum* written in 2012/13, I argued that the most likely outcome of the current process would be a form of federalism, where Scotland gains substantial economic autonomy while remaining nominally in the United Kingdom. Actually, what I advocated was something called "independence in the UK", which was a phrase Donald Dewar once used in the 1980s. This may seem a contradiction in terms, but constitutionalism is replete with oxymorons and ambiguities. This one at least recognises that in many ways Scotland is already more than just a federal or provincial unit of government, having retained much of its national and institutional identity after the 1707 Union. Scotland never ceased to be a nation.

This Union, in my view, and of many Scottish voters, is past its sell-by date, but Scots are not natural revolutionaries, and they rarely take to the streets. Over the last forty years they have always proceeded legally, consensually, incrementally through progressive devolution. This was the way the Scottish

Parliament was restored after 300 years, an institution that is now central to Scottish public life. Back in 2012, I saw no logical reason why this should not continue towards a new multinational UK in which Scotland had a large measure of economic and legislative autonomy while still remaining within the UK. New wine in old bottles.

After all, I argued, if Scotland were to become independent, it would on day one have to set about creating cross border entities to manage the common problems that would face both countries, locked together as they are on this small island off Europe. Everything from monetary policy to immigration; marine conservation to renewable energy; defence cooperation to the BBC. Geography is destiny, I said, and it made little sense for Scotland to try to split off from the archipelago. And following this reasoning, does it not make sense for Scotland to continue to send elected representatives to the quasi-federal centre, London, where so many decisions crucial to Scotland's welfare will be decided? This all seemed to make a clear case for federalism rather than independence. So, why did I end up voting Yes in the referendum? For three reasons.

Firstly, it seemed clear to me that while Scotland saw the need for a federal reshaping of the UK constitution, it was also clear that England did not. There may be Southern grievances about Scotland's alleged excessive subsidies through the Barnett Formula, and about Scottish MPs voting on English matters when English MPs don't enjoy reciprocal rights in Holyrood. English regions feel remote from Westminster. Cities in the North of England have been campaigning for a better deal, including tax raising powers, and of course, London now has a very combative mayor arguing for more autonomy. But these tensions have never been enough to move the English voters as a whole – who constitute 80% of the UK electorate – to seek a coherent federal solution, with a separation of powers, a written constitution, regional parliaments, a Senate and a new federal level of government. Regional devolution was decisively rejected by the North in referendums in 2004. The trouble is that England is quite happy with its parliament: it is called the House of Commons.

I still believe this to be the case, despite the Prime Minister David Cameron's "alarm call" at 7am on the morning after the referendum when he said that further Scottish devolution would have to go "in tandem" with English Votes for English Laws (EVEL).

Excluding Scots MP from voting on nominally English bills in the House of Commons is not federalism, nor is it particularly radical. David Cameron was not proposing a constitutional convention; merely trying to put Ed Miliband in a hole by edging Labour out of government in England. England has yet to be convinced that it needs a new constitution or indeed any codified document expressly dividing sovereignty.

My second reason for voting Yes was the publication of the Scottish Government's Independence White Paper in November 2013. It was clear from this voluminous document that the Scottish government was not talking about independence any more in any recognisable sense. No declaration of independence runs to 670 pages – the American Declaration of Independence got the thrust of its argument on one broadsheet page, as did the Declaration of Arbroath. The SNP abandoned separatism in 1989 when it adopted the policy of independence in Europe which already implies ceding of sovereignty to Brussels. But the White Paper took this much further indicating that Scotland would retain a common currency after independence, which would constrain economic autonomy, not least because the Bank of England would be setting interest rates, controlling borrowing, and possibly even aspects of taxation.[ii]

The Queen would remain Head of State, the BBC would continue in some form, Scotland's defence infrastructure (Trident excluded) would remain integrated with the UK's, and of course Scotland would remain with the UK in NATO. The White Paper also made clear that medical and academic research would continue on a UK basis, along with energy subsidies, pension funds and bank regulation. The National Lottery, the National Health Service, the National Grid, the foreign diplomatic service would continue. Scotland would remain in the UK's Common Travel Area, which implied a common immigration policy and a rejection of the Shengen passport free zone. The White Paper even said that a future Scottish government would support the UK's continuing seat in the United Nations Security Council.

This indy-lite was so light it had to be tethered to the ground or it would blow away. Just what would change after independence? Not even the headings on Scottish Government notepaper. Alex

---

ii The Governor of the Bank of England made this clear to the TUC as "some form of fiscal arrangement. You need tax, revenues and spending flowing across those borders" (9/9/14).

Salmond insisted that people would still call themselves British and the Yes Campaign argued that the United Kingdom would remain, albeit in a new form. Scots could retain their dual identities, there would be no borders and people could even use British passports. There is of course no ethnic or racial dimension – quite rightly – to Scottish nationalism, so it is not even as if there would be a cultural transformation of Scotland in a less English direction. English history would not be down-graded in schools to make way for Scottish folk tales. This looked to me like a federalist project, or more properly a confederalist project that would mean that calling for actual federalism was otiose. We might as well call it independence and be done with it.

But the final nail in the Unionist coffin for this writer, and the third and probably most important reason I voted Yes, was the Chancellor George Osborne's Declaration on the Pound in February 2013. As explained in earlier chapters, this indicated to me that the Union of which Scotland believed itself to be a member had fundamentally changed. It was no longer a partnership of nations but instead placed Scotland in a new position of regional subordination. If Westminster was claiming that the common currency of the UK – the pound – was now exclusively English property, then it seemed to me that the old Unionist bargain, if it ever existed, had ceased. This was no longer a union of equals: it even amounted, in monetary terms at least, to something more like retrospective annexation. This is not a relationship of equality and I believe this has been borne out by recent post-referendum experience.

I ended up voting Yes to independence to get a new improved United Kingdom – one that was explicitly based on the self-determination of the nations of which it was composed. It just seemed simpler and clearer for Scotland to make the break, make its implicit sovereignty explicit, establish the ground rules, and then rejoin a federal UK from a position of strength rather than as a subordinate region. I did not believe that the UK would proceed with its monetary exclusion of Scotland, damaging English trade as much as Scottish, and I don't believe in their heart of hearts many economists seriously believed it would either. Nor did I think that Europe and NATO would reject Scotland's continued membership; far from it. NATO would be even more eager for Scotland, given its strategic location vis-à-vis Russia, to remain in the fold. The EU would have been foolish to expel a country which has been subject to EU law for 20 years and has most of Europe's oil and gas reserves. There was, and is, far greater risk of Scotland finding itself out of the European Union by remaining with the UK, given the rising tide of anti-Europeanism, UKIP, and David Cameron's promise of an in/out referendum in 2017.

The more I thought about it, the more it seemed to make sense to remake the United Kingdom holistically, rather than through piecemeal constitutional tinkering with Scotland's relations with the UK. The experience of the referendum campaign only reinforced this conviction, which I had formed when independence still only seemed a remote possibility. Witnessing Scotland's political and constitutional awakening during the campaign seemed to me to make the case for self-government unanswerable. Hundreds of thousands of people had taken possession of the democratic process and asserted their right to live in a better, fairer society. The country has moved on from baby-step devolution. Scotland has always been a nation, but it had rediscovered itself, was confident of its values, and independence seemed to be only a matter of time.

BACK TO THE FUTURE

However, the Scottish people – most of them – thought otherwise. Scotland voted No to independence and we are where we are, at least for the time being. Voters, older ones at any rate, believed that seeking independence without the blessing of the rest of the UK would be fraught with dangers and unquantifiable risks. People believed that their pensions would be hammered, that mortgage rates would rise, that businesses would leave, and that the Scottish Government would suffer a financial crisis as Holyrood's relatively high public spending was caught in the vice of Scotland's ageing population and dwindling oil revenues. Moreover, they believed the protestations from Unionists that there would be significant further powers devolved to the Scottish Parliament if the Scots voted No. The famous "Vow" on the front page of the *Daily Record* indicated that further devolution would come within six months and that it would not damage Scotland financially through any abandonment of the Barnett Formula. It was Project Vow, as much as Project Fear, that turned the opinion polls in the dying days of the campaign. A majority of Scots decided that it was better to stick with the devil they knew.

So I fear we are back in the dry-as-dust world of constitutional scholasticism, of devolution, regionalism, and asymmetrical federalism. There has been an entire academic industry built up over the last four decades in the wake of Scotland's home rule movements. Based around hubs like Nuffield College Oxford, and the Constitution Unit at UCL, a small army of predominantly Unionist academics, like Professors Alan Trench, Jim Gallagher, Iain McLean and Adam Tomkins, have been slicing and dicing the UK constitution along with think tankers like Guy Lodge of the Institute for Public Policy in the Regions. They spend their time at academic conferences discussing answers to the Scottish Question; devolution plus, devolution more, devolution this, devolution that. And as the Smith Commission on further powers for Holyrood got down to work in the weeks following the referendum, it looked like back to business as usual.

Expectations of the Smith Commission were never high, even among many Unionists. For a start, Lord Smith of Kelvin may have been a very competent organiser of the Glasgow Commonwealth Games, but that hardly equipped him to conduct a constitutional review of this magnitude and historical significance. Anyway, as a member of an unelected upper house, owing his peerage to the Westminster political establishment, he was hardly the ideal figure to fashion a new constitution for the United Kingdom which would have involved the scrapping of the very House of Lords in which he sits. Nevertheless, Lord Smith proceeded efficiently and fairly, within the terms of his remit, and began what could only ever be a hasty pork-barrel compromise between the Scottish parties.

Political parties are there to win elections, and the various representatives on the Commission knew that their first responsibility was not to the people of Scotland but to the careers of their members of parliament, present and future. Labour wanted to outflank the Scottish Nationalists, who had seen an extraordinary explosion in their membership, and reassert their grip on Scottish politics and public sector patronage. The Scottish Tories wanted to introduce a radical tax-cutting agenda to Scotland in order to revive what they regard as latent Conservative support among the Scottish middle-classes. The Scottish National Party under its new leader, Nicola Sturgeon, wanted to show that it was not standing aloof as it had in the past from the constitutional reform process, while avoiding any scheme that would force them to cut public spending in the run-up to the 2016 Holyrood elections. The Green Party was, of course, ignored.

The most obvious omission from this constitutional process was Scottish civil society, the extra-parliamentary movement that had provided the moral impetus behind the restoration of the Scottish Parliament and compelled the parties to look beyond their narrow interests.

BREAKING WITH CONVENTION

The Scottish Constitutional Convention in the 1980s and 90s not only mobilised public opinion and gave voice to the various non-parliamentary interest groups like third sector charities, trades unions, churches: it also wrote the blueprint for the new Scottish Parliament. And did it rather well. The reason we have a Scottish legislature with primary law-making powers, elected under proportional representation, with a commitment to consensus rather than adversarialism is because civic representatives, like the journalist Joyce McMillan, the Labour MP Henry McLeish and the former Scottish civil servant Jim Ross, toiled on the Consultative Steering Group. It was the Convention that, in 1989, managed to persuade all of Scotland's Labour MPs – bar Tam Dalyell – to sign a pledge that sovereignty would be returned to the Scottish people. A remarkable constitutional moment the significance of which is perhaps only now becoming apparent. It read:

> We, gathered as the Scottish Constitutional Convention, do hereby acknowledge the sovereign right of the Scottish people to determine the form of Government best suited to their needs, and do hereby declare and pledge that in all our actions and deliberations their interests shall be paramount.
> Signed: Alistair Darling, George Robertson, Gordon Brown et al.

It had no legal force at the time and was dismissed by "She who must be obeyed" – Margaret Thatcher – as irrelevant, self-appointed and unrepresentative. But sometimes words really are powerful weapons, and within a decade, a Scottish parliament was restored with primary law making powers.

There was, of course, no time after the independence referendum to set up another constitutional convention for Scotland before the Smith Commission met. I suggested, rather cheekily, that the various groups, including the STUC, SCVO, Yes Scotland, National Collective, Bella Caledonia, Common Weal, should form a pop-up convention along with think tanks like Reform Scotland, and try to get civic Scotland levered into the Smith Commission. Lord Smith had agreed that civic Scotland should "have a say" in the process, but I argued in my own submission that they should actually be properly represented if the Commission was to have legitimacy.

I had suggested that someone like Joyce McMillan, the distinguished Yes-supporting journalist, might have been the kind of person who could have been co-opted onto Smith. She had experience of home rule movements, not least in Eastern Europe, in addition to her role on the original Constitutional Convention steering group that drafted the constitutional principles of the Scottish Parliament. In an article in the *Sunday Herald*, I also nominated Henry McLeish, the No-voting former Labour First Minister, who had done most of the leg-work on the 1998 Scotland Bill and who was a firm advocate of devolution max. I wasn't expecting this to be taken entirely seriously. Nevertheless, I still believe that if people like these had been present on the Smith Commission representing civic Scotland, this might have swung the balance and prevented it becoming wholly owned property of the political parties. They certainly could have formed a powerful, indeed decisive, home rule bloc with the Greens, the Liberal Democrats and the SNP MPs represented.

But the task of achieving constitutional consensus turned out to be harder than in the 1980s, in part because of the very vigour of the grass roots campaign that had developed so much momentum before the referendum. In the weeks and months following the vote, movements sprang up all over Scotland calling themselves things like Voice of the People, Hope Against Fear, The 45, which latter was not only a reference to the percentage who voted Yes but also an allusion to the Jacobite Rebellion of 1745. Within weeks of the result thousands of people started gathering outside the Scottish Parliament demanding a "revote" - three thousand on September 27th alone.

There was a widespread sense of betrayal among many of the independence cadres, and 94,000 signed a petition alleging that the voting had been rigged in the election, a claim that was vigorously rejected by the chief counting officer Mary Pitcaithly. It would have been hard to corral these groups into a convention – pop up or otherwise – seeking, not independence, but a better form of home rule. Many activists had been gripped by the prospect of another early referendum on the basis that the Scottish people had been "lied to" by the Unionist parties. Many activists on social media made clear they believed that the referendum was null and void. The "lies" ranged from the allegation that older pensioners had been told by Better Together canvassers that their pensions would be lost after independence, to the claim that the discovery of a huge new oil field off Shetland was being kept secret from the Scottish public.

Naturally, the *Daily Record*'s "Vow" was seen as a mendacious fix from Unionists trying to dupe the Scots with promises of devolution max that were never going to be delivered. Many of The 45 tendency wanted nothing more to do with the UK state and wanted to go for full independence – nothing less. There were calls for the SNP to avoid referendums and to make a Unilateral Declaration of Independence after the next Scottish parliamentary elections. The former leader of the SNP, Gordon Wilson, in his book *Scotland: Battle for Independence*, said that "coyness on national identity" by Yes had lost the referendum and that the SNP had been naive to pursue a constitutional road.

The more thoughtful Yes groups like the Common Weal, led by Robin McAlpine, had no objection to the constitutional convention idea as such, or to putting pressure on the Smith Commission. Common Weal made a submission calling for all tax and welfare to be devolved to Holyrood. But many believed the real struggle had moved on. Scotland was no longer prepared to put its faith in the "great and the good" and McAlpine and others wanted to continue building on the strength of radical grass-roots activism. Few believed that Smith was capable of coming up with any substantial measure of home rule, and that it would be a diversion of effort to arouse peoples' hopes. Better to concentrate on building a continuing independence campaign that could destroy the so-called "Red Tories" of the Scottish Labour Party.

Many Labour constituencies, in Glasgow, North Lanarkshire and Dundee had voted Yes, and activists in the Common Weal believed that it would be possible to use tactical voting in the 2015 general election to have Labour removed. Common Weal and others flirted with the idea of setting up a new party, like the Greek Syriza, as a coalition of the radical left in Scotland, but this was abandoned on the grounds that the SNP, under Nicola Sturgeon, had a broadly social democratic outlook. A new party would have split the independence vote and the preferred route was some kind of electoral pact or Yes Alliance.

Alex Salmond had ruled out another referendum "for a generation, if not a lifetime". However, he was no longer in charge and hopes rose that public pressure might force a referendum earlier than that. My view was that another referendum was unlikely because the Scottish and UK governments would have to agree to hold one, and the SNP was still very wary of the idea. If they sought to break Salmond's promise and foist another on Scotland, they would certainly lose it and then lose power in the 2016 Scottish Parliamentary election. The new leader of the Scottish National Party, Nicola Sturgeon, was only too aware of the risk of getting carried away with the idea of another referendum and has consistently said she is not planning for one. (Mind you, when politicians say that it usually means they're not completely ruling it out). The SNP had decided to accept the referendum and to look for ways of promoting home rule. In *The Observer* (29/9/14), Sturgeon made her bargaining position clear:

> In the final days of the campaign, the Unionist parties made a solemn promise, styled as a vow, to the people of Scotland. The language used around that was of devo max or something close to federalism or home rule. This took it beyond the detail of what these parties had previously offered. This was something that was going to markedly change the ability of the Scottish Parliament to deliver on the economy and on welfare. And so this is what now needs to be defined and delivered. This is where people are in their expectations.

The politician largely responsible for generating these great expectations, as discussed earlier, was the former Prime Minister, Gordon Brown. In his speech in Loanhead on 9th September 2014, he had said that "the plan for a stronger Scottish Parliament we seek agreement on is for nothing else than a modern form of Scottish Home Rule within the United Kingdom". Newspapers reported this as "Scottish Independence: Gordon Brown pledges new Home Rule Bill" (*Press and Journal* 9/9/14). He also wrote in the New York Times that "the United Kingdom is moving as close to a federal state as is possible". He said that Scotland would, if it voted No, receive powers that would be "as near to federalism as is possible in a nation where one part forms 85% of the population".

Brown also appeared to be talking about federalism in his book *My Scotland, Our Britain* published in the run-up to the referendum, in which he said that there should be a new power and tax-sharing union between Scotland and the UK with an explicit division of powers. Many commentators picked up his argument, such as Will Hutton in *The Observer*: "Only a commitment to a fully fledged constitutional convention to discuss how to federalise Britain" he said, "will now stop the Yes campaign in Scotland." Commentators in Scotland like David Torrance said that federalism was coming to Scotland after a No vote. "Brown's plan for the UK" he said in *The Herald*, "is federalism in all but name" (15/6/14).

Since the referendum, the Unionist parties have insisted that there was never any pledge from any one of federalism or devolution max, which is essentially a unilateral version of it. The Tory leader, Ruth Davidson told the Conservative Party Conference in October 2014 that "devo max is a non starter". Gordon Brown appears to have lost his enthusiasm for federalism and argued in the Commons on 16th October 2014 that even tax devolution would be "a lethal cocktail", and that devolution max would be "a Trojan horse" for independence. The shadow of Lord Home hangs heavily over Brown in they eyes of many Yes voters. However, the federal cat is out of the bag, and it is not going to be put back.

I argued in my submission to Smith that anything less than devolution max is likely to be seen by many in Scotland as a betrayal of the democratic process. We need only look at Northern Ireland to see what happens when the democratic process breaks down and people start to take matters into their own hands. I am not saying that Scotland could descend into civil war. This is a very different country, as I have tried to emphasise elsewhere in this book. Scots do not take to the streets readily and they abhor militant politics. They resisted the poll tax peacefully and democratically in the 1980s, even though it was the Battle of Trafalgar Square in 1990 that forced the Conservatives to scrap it. And in the decades since they have continued to deploy the ballot box rather than the paving stone, or still less, the bullet. However, the large number of people in Scotland who have now lost confidence entirely in Westminster will not remain passive for long. If the expectations that Nicola Sturgeon referred to are not met, it is quite possible that some might call for a campaign of civil disobedience or a refusal to pay taxes.

The various organisations that grew out of the independence campaign have now come together in a general demand for home rule – at least as a staging post to independence. Nicola Sturgeon has continued in the gradualist mould of her predecessor and has put her efforts into securing further devolution. She is explicitly seeking a form of unilateral federalism as outlined in the SNP's submission to the Smith Commission, which even quotes Gordon Brown's remarks.[44] It seems as if, for the time being, federalism is the only game in town for the independence movement. But what exactly does federalism mean?

FEDERALISM IN ONE COUNTRY?

Federalism is a system of government in which sovereignty is not centralised but is shared; it is divided across states or provinces. In all federal systems, there is a written constitution or a codification of the explicit division of responsibilities between the federal government and the states of the Union. There are democratic legislatures both at the centre and in the member states with primary law making powers and wide latitude on taxation. There is usually an upper chamber, or senate, which acts as a regional revising chamber, and a supreme court to adjudicate on disputes between the various levels of government. Further than that, there are mechanisms for raising taxation at federal level and state level and formulae for redistributing revenues from wealthier states to less wealthy ones.

The key difference between federalism and a unitary state is that the subordinate legislatures cannot be abolished. The Greater London Council, for example, was a creation of Westminster and it was abolished by Margaret Thatcher in 1986. Had it been a federal unit of government, it would not have been possible to abolish the GLC. The abolition of the Scottish Parliament may seem a remote eventuality, but it is still possible. This is why even Gordon Brown said that there should be a declaration of sovereignty so that what is immutable can be clearly stated as such. It needs to be spelled out that that the Scottish Parliament exercises sovereignty, not delegated responsibility.

But Britain remains, even after devolution, constitutionally a unitary state. Many academics dispute this, and say that it is a "union state", a "multinational state" or a "plurinational state". And they are right to say that, with devolution of power to the Scottish Parliament and to Wales, the UK does not behave as a unitary state in the old, monolithic sense that was understood by the Victorian constitutionalist AV Dicey. He saw sovereignty as something mystical and indivisible, like monarchy itself. But the fact that Holyrood makes laws does not mean that the UK is a federal state – far from it. As the late Enoch Powell pointed out, power devolved is power retained. The Scottish Parliament may appear to exercise sovereignty, but it is still a creature of Westminster. The Scotland Act 1998 is very clear that "Westminster remains sovereign in all matters". Every act of the Scottish Parliament has to be ratified by Westminster, and signed off by the Queen. This is no mere formality. It confirms that the central principle of the UK constitution is a unitary one: it is based on parliamentary sovereignty.

So what specific powers does each level of sovereign government exercise in a federal system? This can vary enormously, but the bottom line is always that defence, foreign affairs, monetary policy, and overall economic management are functions retained for the federal level of government. Domestic affairs like policing, education and health etc. are generally organised at state or regional level. Taxation is generally shared between the two. But even in America, which is one of the most centralised federations in the world, there are states which have remarkably wide latitude to go their own way. Oregon has abolished sales taxes and uses income tax solely to finance its activities, which include having the highest minimum wage in the Union.

In Canada, federal provinces are constitutionally able to tax anything they want to tax, except international and internal trade, setting their own rates, using their own definitions of tax bases, and collecting taxes themselves.[45] The state of Quebec has economic powers so extensive that under the SNP's definition, it is already practically independent, while remaining a part of the Canadian federation. It is one of the most social democratic societies in North America, with Nordic levels of social protection within a market economy.

For example, Quebec has pioneered universal day care at a bargain basement charge of $7 dollars a day. Child care was the centre-piece policy in the Scottish Government's White Paper, in which it was argued that near-free child care could only come with independence. Not so. When Quebec voted narrowly to stay in the Canadian Union in 1995, it was not voting to remain in a country in which economic policy was dominated by a centralised state like the one we have in Westminster. The issue of independence remains a live one in Quebec, even though the language issue has largely been resolved. However, it is principally now about whether Quebec should have its own defence and foreign policy. Just about everything else is devolved.

If Britain introduced federalism, then Westminster, or a federal legislature, would have powers over military deployment, war-making, defence expenditure and international relations such as membership of NATO. This is one of the main objections to federalism put forward by supporters of Scottish independence. Scotland could have a moral voice, of course, and would be free to campaign for the removal of Trident or against illegal wars. But there should be no ambiguities here: in federal unions, defence and the security of the state against foreign incursion is the central responsibility of the federal level. Indeed, in Canada, it was fear about the American War of Independence spilling over into Canada that led the first President, the Glaswegian, John Macdonald, to argue successfully for Canada to become a federal union in the 1860s.

In a federal constitution, the UK would also have full control of monetary policy, overall economic policy, subject to negotiation with the provincial parliaments. This also makes federalism objectionable to many nationalists who say that Scotland could never be called independent when it allows much of its economic policy to be dictated by Westminster. Mind you, even the Scottish

Government accepted the principle of fiscal federalism in the White Paper on independence. It agreed that interest rates and overall borrowing would be regulated by the central, federal bank – the Bank of England. In a federal system the central government would also have its own tax base to finance those activities, like defence, which it must conduct on behalf of the entire federation, and to secure financial stability.

Scotland is already a considerable way down the road to federalism, or home rule. It has a democratically elected parliament with primary law-making powers over domestic legislation. It also has tax-raising powers which it has never used, mainly because they were limited to varying only the basic rate of income tax. The principle that Holyrood should widen its powers to levy taxation to fund most of its services was made by the Calman Commission in 2009. Labour has always held back from adopting fiscal autonomy, according to its submission to the Smith Commission, because it would undermine the principle of sharing in what Gordon Brown calls the "welfare union". He argued that for this pooling of resources to take place, the vast majority of taxes must be raised at the centre and then disbursed through some spending formula like the Barnett Formula.

However, there is no logical reason why a federal Scotland should not have a full range of taxation options at its disposal as part of a federal UK – oil revenues for example, or excise duties, corporation tax, inheritance tax, national insurance. Scotland remains the only region, state, or principality in the world to have discovered oil in its waters and not had any direct benefit from it. In the state of Alaska, for example, the governor allocates a dividend to each citizen each year related to oil revenues. In Alberta, Canada, hydrocarbon wealth is diverted into a pension fund.

There has been tax sharing, certainly, in a federal system, and all states have a responsibility to avoid both social dumping and a race to the bottom through irresponsible taxation and welfare policies. However, it seems perfectly reasonable for Scotland and other regions of the UK to adjust corporation tax to try to keep business from migrating south. These are matters that can be negotiated in federal systems. Similarly, borrowing powers can be devolved in federal systems, even though the overall limits would have to be managed on a UK-wide basis. In Canada, states have wide powers to issue bonds, and have full access to domestic and international capital markets.

In such systems, there are also mechanisms to effect redistribution between states. Where they exist, they are mostly non-controversial or at least do not dominate public debate in the way the Barnett Formula does in the UK. For example, when I visited the state parliament in Melbourne, Australia, my queries about tax, funding formulas and distribution were met with bemused smiles by journalists and politicians. They told me that no one is remotely interested in stuff which happens in smoke-less rooms filled with bureaucrats using crazy formulas no one understands. In Quebec, there is a similar response if you start asking how cross funding takes place. Here is the formula used in Canada:

equalization province $J(>0)$

$$= \left[\sum_{i=1}^{N} \left[\left(\begin{array}{c} \text{per capita} \\ \text{tax base } i \\ \text{standard} \end{array} - \begin{array}{c} \text{per capita} \\ \text{tax base } i \\ \text{province } J \end{array} \right) \times \begin{array}{c} \text{average} \\ \text{tax} \\ \text{rate } i \end{array} \right] \right] \times \begin{array}{c} \text{population} \\ \text{province } J \end{array},$$

Now, of course, there are disputes about money in federal systems and on the distribution of revenues. Small states with low tax bases feel disadvantaged. But these are not seen as constitutional issues but as matters for negotiation between sovereign entities. The reason taxation is such a hot issue in the UK is because it is a battleground over the constitutional limits of the ill-defined powers of the Scottish Parliament.

In my submission to the Smith Commission, I argued that once the sovereignty of the Scottish Parliament is clearly defined, the rest of the devolution max can be deduced by applying the principle of subsidiarity – that only those powers which must be held at the centre are held there. This is the principle which informed the Scotland Act 1998. Only the powers reserved to Westminster are specified in the Act and everything else is assumed to be the responsibility of Holyrood. Unless there is a very compelling reason for not giving a tax power to Scotland, as is the case with VAT, trade tariffs or some excise duties, it should be assumed that Holyrood has the power to levy it. This would make the Scottish Parliament properly accountable and allow its governments the power to use taxation constructively to achieve social and economic objectives.

Similarly, applying the principle of subsidiarity, it makes little sense for matters like broadcasting and abortion to be reserved powers for Westminster. Scotland has its own political system, historical institutions, and culture, and needs a broadcasting system that reflects this. This does not mean that Scottish politicians should interfere with editorial decisions in the BBC, any more than MPs currently do in Westminster. But overall regulation of broadcasting should clearly lie with the Scottish Parliament. And when criminal justice, family law, health, education and marriage are devolved by what reasoning is abortion reserved to Westminster?

Devolution max is simply subsidiarity in practice. However, prominent Unionist academics like the former civil servant Professor Jim Gallagher, who say they favour change and agree that federalism is a workable system, nevertheless draw the line at applying devolution max to Scotland. He describes it in *The Day After Judgement*, as "a botched form of independence".[46] Yet he goes on to say that he favours a form of federal state with "a single external face, a fully integrated economy and a high degree of social solidarity". Later, he adds the principle of subsidiarity to the mix, arguing that power should be "decentralised unless there is a good reason to retain power at a higher level". It seems to me that, if you follow those principles, you get to federalism. But unfortunately, in the post-referendum period, federalism and devolution max have come to be seen as inherently nationalist policies, and therefore on the dark side and to be dismissed. In the tribal world of Scottish politics, anything that the SNP supports must be attacked at all costs.

The usual argument against federalism is that it is impossible in a country where 85% of the population live in one part of it. That is true. But the history of devolution shows that it is quite possible to disaggregate the powers of the UK state incrementally and in an asymmetrical way. The Scottish Parliament has very considerable powers and it has increased them significantly in the years since its creation in 1999, but the sky hasn't fallen in. What has happened is that other parts of the UK, like Wales, have seen the value of self-determination and have decided to demand it themselves. It is true that the formal institutions of a fully federal state do not yet exist in the UK. There is no Senate, no written constitution, no supreme court, no regional parliaments, no federal level of government – and there is no sign of these being introduced in the near future. But it is not in Scotland's power to impose these institutions on a reluctant United Kingdom. And just as Scotland cannot dictate to the rest of the UK how fast it moves in this federal direction, nor should the rest of the UK set arbitrary limits to the devolution of power to Scotland.

So, federalism is a perfectly respectable and rational system of government for a multinational state like Britain. However, as I argue later, it may be that the federal moment has passed for the United Kingdom. The momentum generated by the independence movement is taking Scotland so far down the road of self-government that it may no longer be possible to halt it, or contain it within a new federal constitution even if one were on offer. And it certainly appears that the talk of federalism before the referendum was not entirely serious. With hindsight, it looks as if Gordon Brown's cryptic remarks, like the editorials in the UK press on federalism, were part of the general attempt by Unionists to head off a Yes vote by hinting at a new constitutional settlement, much as Lord Home promised Scots a better devolution if they voted No in 1979. No doubt the constitutional lawyers and academics will continue to propose new forms of devolution to contain the demands, not just of Scotland, but other parts of the UK. Devolution plus, minus and squared. That is what constitutionalists are there for. The reforms proposed by the Smith Commission will no doubt take the Scottish Parliament a few steps further down the road to self-determination. But there seems little likelihood that they will resolve the Scottish question, or satisfy demands for home rule.

There is a limit to how much federal constitutional radicalism the UK voters can take. Most English voters say they want English votes for English laws, but they are instinctively hostile to tinkering with Westminster to set up the apparatus of a fully federal constitution. What does seem most likely is that the voting rights of Scottish MPs in Westminster will be curbed, and the Barnett Formula reformed or scrapped. It may be that Scotland will again face the choice, in a decade or two, of whether to remain in the UK or to leave, and thereafter perhaps to seek a looser, confederal arrangement in a different United Kingdom. I suspect it will make a different choice to the one it made in September 2014.

CHAPTER SEVEN

The Queer Fish – From Salmond to Sturgeon

On the afternoon following the referendum defeat, Alex Salmond summoned the Scottish press corps – or most of them – to the state room in his official residence, Bute House, in Edinburgh's New Town. Before its ornate rococo mirror he announced that he would be standing down as First Minister: "As leader my time is nearly over... but for Scotland the campaign continues and the dream shall never die." It was one of the more graceful departures in modern British politics from a man regarded by many commentators as a singularly graceless politician. He was clearly shocked by the scale of the referendum defeat and had realised in the early hours of Friday morning that politics in Scotland had changed. Alex Salmond decided that the best thing he could do for his party was to remove himself from the firing line; the better to place David Cameron firmly in it.

Salmond is famously a gambler – an aficionado of the turf – and he had quit while he was ahead. There was no immediate pressure to go. He had not been defeated in any parliamentary election and his standing in the opinion polls remained high, as did the popularity of the SNP. He'd just lost a referendum but delivered an impressive result, with nearly half the Scottish adult population supporting independence. But he was wise not to overstay his welcome. Political leaders tend to cling to office until they are dragged out kicking and screaming, fingernails dug into the door-frame. But Salmond knew that much of his authority had been damaged and he saw an opportunity to exit history on his own terms, at a time of his choosing.

The initial reaction from the press corps was a stunned silence. Most journalists had expected Salmond to go, but not immediately, not now. You could almost hear the room thinking: "for heaven's sake, we haven't had time to cut him down to size yet". Later, the *Daily Mail* led the assault: "You were either on his side or against him", it said of his departure, "Critics were dismissed as scaremongers. Facts dismissed as lies, experts flatly ignored. That was how he ran things." It was rather childish of Salmond to ban the *Daily Mail* from his resignation press briefing, but it was understandable. When successful democratic politicians leave office, there is usually an attempt to find at least a few kind words. But Alex Salmond's departure was hailed by some as little short of a liberation from tyranny. The former *Daily Record* political editor, Chris Deerin, gave this valedictory:

> The departure of Alex Salmond removes from the scene a cynical, bloodless card sharp. It's perhaps too much to compare his exit to the death of an evil Disney queen, where the curse is lifted and the frozen land returns to its old, verdant, sun-dappled beauty, its citizens dancing in golden cobbled streets – but there is undoubtedly a sense of clouds parting, of a boot being removed from the nation's throat.

There has never been much affection between the Scottish press and Alex Salmond. Headlines like these during the referendum campaign told readers all they needed to know about how journalists regarded the First Minister of Scotland: "Bare-faced liar: Alex Salmond's reputation in the mud" (*Politics.co.uk*); "Desperate Alex Salmond will say anything to con Scottish voters", (*Sunday Express*); "Salmond's All Snarls as he shows his true colours" (*Daily Telegraph*). "Salmond is like Hitler, says Starkey" (*Independent*). Commentators in the UK press tended to regard him as a dangerous demagogue. Even liberals, like *The Guardian*'s Michael White, referred to Salmond as "wily", "devious", and "slippery", while on *Newsnight* Jeremy Paxman once compared the First Minister to Robert Mugabe.

It has never been entirely clear why Salmond aroused quite such strong antagonism among the press because, like him or loathe him, he has always been good copy, forever ready with a quotable sound bite. Indeed, in his resignation statement he coined at least two: he said that the referendum result was "redolent with opportunities for Scotland and the Scottish National Party" and that he would "hold Westminster's feet to the fire" over their promises of extensive new powers for the Scottish Parliament. In fact, though no one realised, those two phrases amounted to a mission statement for his return to front line politics under a different guise.

The Scottish people, on the whole, did not seem to buy the press's image of Salmond, even if they regarded him as someone with, as is said in Scotland, "a guid conceit of himself". On the eve of his departure from Bute House the First Minister was vastly more popular in Scotland than any of the UK leaders, having an approval rating in Scotland of plus 11. David Cameron had a rating of minus 45, Ed Miliband minus 46 and Nick Clegg minus 53.[47] Remarkably, Alex Salmond had a positive approval rating throughout his seven years as First Minister of Scotland. Most political leaders experience long periods of mid-term unpopularity – but not him. Indeed, most of his time in office, Salmond had been more popular than all the Scottish opposition leaders combined. Even in June 2014, after months of criticism in the press over his policies on Europe and the pound, Ipsos/Mori recorded his approval rating at 49%, against the Labour leader Johann Lamont on 38%, the Tories' Ruth Davidson at 32% and the Liberal Democrat leader, Willie Rennie, on 20%.[48] Salmond's popularity in Scotland actually rose after he resigned, another first for one of the longest serving party leaders since Gladstone.

Salmond defied the laws of political gravity by cultivating a double image: head of the Scottish Government but also as guardian of Scotland against the predations of Westminster. He managed to be in office and in opposition simultaneously. Salmond would congratulate his government for delivering improved employment figures, and then attack Westminster for undermining the economy – sometimes in the same speech. He was never much of a hit with women, however. A Survation poll for the *Daily Record* in August 2014 held a sobering message for the Yes campaign.[49] It confirmed that the words most women voters associate with Alex Salmond are "arrogant", "ambitious" and "dishonest". This is intriguing because many of them must have nevertheless voted for him in Holyrood. The instant negative reaction given to opinion pollsters may in part be a reflection of the largely negative way Salmond is portrayed in the press.

Salmond's greatest achievement however was not his own popularity but the enduring success of the Scottish National Party. He won the party's first ever election in 2007, delivered a landslide in 2011, and, after the referendum defeat in 2014, the SNP was still recording Scottish opinion poll ratings in excess of 40% for Holyrood and even for Westminster. This means even after losing to Better Together, the SNP was still on course to win the next Scottish parliamentary elections by almost as large a margin as in 2011. Some opinion polls after the referendum suggested that the SNP had even displaced Labour as Scotland's party of choice in

Westminster. The most extraordinary was a YouGov poll for STV that put the SNP on 52% for the general election against Labour on 23%. It was the continuing popularity of Salmond and his party that led most in the press to believe he would hang around as First Minister.

Was he pushed? No. Salmond's authority in the party was as high as ever, despite the loss of the referendum. His successor, Nicola Sturgeon, was certainly champing at the bit, and had a successful referendum campaign. But no one in the SNP is strong enough to have pushed Alex Salmond out of the door, physically or politically, and she would never have tried. He had left of his own accord once before, in 2000, and his party practically begged him to return. When he finally did, adopting Nicola Sturgeon as his deputy, he proceeded to consolidate his hold on Scottish politics by promoting a raft of popular policies, like the abolition of university tuition fees and opposition to the Iraq war, which positioned the SNP to the left of Labour.

Labour has traditionally dominated Scottish politics, and sent 41 out of 59 Scottish MPs to Westminster in 2010, on the strength of over a million Scottish votes. However, Salmond's outflanking of its indifferent leadership in Holyrood, plus his obvious determination to fight Scotland's corner, led to the remarkable breakthrough which triggered the independence referendum. In May 2011, the SNP won a majority of seats in a parliament elected on the additional member system – a form of proportional representation which was designed to prevent any party having an absolute majority. Journalists often talk of sensational election results, but this time the superlatives were justified.

The real secret of Salmond's success was party unity – which even some in the SNP have described in recent years as "almost scary". He was described by his predecessor as SNP leader, Gordon Wilson, as an "infant Robespierre", an image originally coined by the former Scottish Secretary, Malcolm Rifkind. The SNP used to be notorious for its internal splits and divisions, but since Salmond became leader it has become docile, almost sheep-like in its willingness to follow its master's bidding. His authority over party structures was such that very little could be done without his agreement; nevertheless, for as long as he made the right calls, this turned the party into a formidable electoral machine. This lack of internal dissent is one reason why Salmond has never been embroiled in scandal despite press suspicion of him. There has been an open cheque book waiting for anyone to come up with a decent scandal about the First Minister – but no one around the party has seen it as being in their interest to collect. In the 25 years since he first became leader of his party in 1990, he has been free of dodgy donations, expenses fiddles, extra-marital affairs, drink problems or any of the many offences that normally lead to shame-faced politicians "spending more time with their families". This is in stark contrast to Labour in Scotland, where rival factions briefing the press have caused countless scandals and in 2008 brought down the Scottish Labour leader, Wendy Alexander, over an unlawful campaign fund donation which only insiders could have known about.

The nearest Salmond came to a real financial scandal was in 2000 when a dispute with the party treasurer, Ian Blackford, led to a series of allegations that Salmond had failed to observe spending limits on his expenses and had taken his wife abroad on SNP funds. But Blackford never succeeded in making any allegations of improper conduct stick and was himself suspended from the party. In 1998, the BBC in London sent a team to Glasgow to investigate Alex Salmond's alleged gambling debts – he was reputed to be under the control of an Irish bookmaker mafia – but they went home empty handed. Salmond was not in the control of anyone, apart possibly from his wife, Moira. When not in his official residence in Edinburgh, Salmond lives quietly in his converted mill in the village of Strichen in Aberdeenshire with his partner of 33 years, who is 17 years his senior and childless. This led to one of the more tasteless assaults on Salmond's character during the referendum campaign. On the 13th September 2014, the *Daily Mail*, ran banner headlines: 'Childless SNP chiefs who have no feel for UK family. Leaders of Scottish National Party want to break up Union because they do not understand families, it is claimed'. The source for this story was a former Scottish international rugby player, not known as an authority on family psychology. It allowed the *Daily Mail* to drag his deputy Nicola Sturgeon into the stew, who is married to the SNP chief executive Peter Murrell, and is also childless.

Salmond is undoubtedly a political obsessive and likes to get his way in the party. Though so long as he kept winning elections, his followers were pretty content to let him have it. A more serious political charge was that while Alex Salmond was brilliant at winning elections in Holyrood, he never succeeded in translating this into victory for independence. Gordon Wilson has criticised him for being a politician of limited vision who could see no further than the next Holyrood election. Some had long suspected that Salmond had lost his belief in pure independence and was content to be the successful manager of a parliament within the United Kingdom.

This strand of criticism resurfaced during the referendum campaign over his reluctance to advocate a separate Scottish currency for an independent Scotland, which meant leaving the Bank of England in charge of interest rates and borrowing in Scotland. A number of figures in Yes Scotland, including the co-chair Denis Canavan, believed this was fundamentally flawed and that Salmond should have been much more positive about sterlingisation – the adoption of an independent Scottish currency pegged to the pound. Wilson also claimed that Salmond's failure on the pound lost the referendum. There are arguments here on both sides. If Salmond had declared currency separatism, the international bond markets would likely have reacted even more negatively, at least in the short term, and he would certainly have been crucified in he press. But there probably should have been more discussion of the issue.

Salmond's authority over his party did become somewhat oppressive in his later years. However, even his strongest detractors had to accept that through gradualism, Alex Salmond's long period as leader had brought Scotland closer to independence than any of his predecessors could ever have dreamed possible. His contribution to Scottish history is immense. Salmond made the Scottish parliament take itself seriously through sheer leadership. His Labour predecessors didn't dare even to call themselves a government. And as he made the Scottish Parliament believe in itself, he helped the Scottish nation rediscover itself. If most Scots now take it as self-evident that Scotland could become one of those successful Nordic countries like Norway and Denmark who combine economic dynamism with high levels of social solidarity, then it is largely down to Alex Salmond. He stopped Scotland thinking of itself as a region.

METHUSELAH

If a week is a long time in politics, then Alex Salmond must be Methuselah, because he had been leader of the Scottish National Party for nearly a quarter of a century, apart from his "sabbatical" in 2000. When he took over the reins, the SNP was a party still in the political wilderness. He had himself been expelled for being a republican socialist member of the '79 group less than a decade previously. Before he was elected National Convenor in September 1990, the SNP had had an indifferent record. It tried, disastrously, to bribe Scots into independence with the crass slogan of "It's Scotland's Oil" in the 1970s. The SNP then practically destroyed itself in 1979 after the abortive devolution referendum by bringing down the Labour government of James Callaghan and forcing an election that not only brought Margaret Thatcher to Number Ten but caused the loss of 11 of the SNP's 13 MPs. Labour never tire of reminding the SNP that they were "the midwives of Thatcherism".

Its most recent miscalculation had been to fail to appreciate the significance of the Scottish Constitutional Convention in 1988 – the cross-party campaign for a Scottish Parliament, which the Nationalists boycotted. Political legend has it that Salmond, by then the young publicity conscious MP for Banff and Buchan, had not been contacted when the decision was made – a claim which is disputed by Jim Sillars, then deputy leader. Salmond began his political life as a protégé of Sillars, a former Labour politician with a robust style. The two never really got on, however, until the 2014 independence referendum campaign, when the hatchet was finally buried.

Most of the traditionalists in the Scottish National Party regarded the young pushy Salmond with suspicion. And they were right to do so. Almost as soon as he took power in September 1990, he abandoned the fundamentalist approach of "independence, nothing less" and sought to place his party in the Scottish political mainstream by supporting devolution. This had previously been regarded by nationalists like Sillars as a Labour trap – a diversion from the true path of independence. But Salmond wasn't really interested in true paths – except those that led to political power. He continued to reposition the SNP as a left of centre rival to the Labour Party and when the opportunity arose to ally with Labour's Donald Dewar after the 1997 Labour election victory in the cause of restoring the Scottish Parliament, he leapt at it.

It was a strange alliance. Donald Dewar never liked dealing with Alex Salmond, and made little secret of his distaste for the Nationalist leader. Nevertheless, the Labour Scottish Secretary found that he needed the SNP leader's support to guarantee that the devolution referendum of 1997 would be a success. It is a mark of how much Salmond had transformed his isolationist party, that he was able to join with Dewar and the Liberal Democrat Jim Wallace in the successful referendum campaign without causing any rebellion in the SNP ranks. In return, Salmond secured from Dewar the famous "deal" that sovereignty would lie in Scotland and not in Westminster. This was a tricky negotiation because Dewar also had to assure his boss Tony Blair that, in the PM's words, "sovereignty would reside with him in Westminster". Dewar squared the circle by arguing that Westminster had exercised sovereignty by delegating sovereignty to the Scottish parliament. Thus began the ambiguity over Holyrood's constitutional status, which remains to this day.

The 1997 devolution referendum was a great victory, with Scots voting for their parliament by a margin of three to one – and also for it to have limited tax powers. Holyrood was given primary legislative power over almost the entire range of domestic policy. Salmond's determination to work with the grain of devolution was finally vindicated in May 1999, when the SNP's veteran Winnie Ewing announced that the Scottish Parliament, adjourned in 1707, was "hereby reconvened". The SNP were not to be early beneficiaries of devolution however. In the 1999 Scottish parliamentary elections, the SNP were marginalised and given very rough treatment by the predominantly Labour-supporting Scottish press, not helped by Salmond's description of the bombing of Belgrade during the Kosovo war as "unpardonable folly". Worse, Salmond discovered that, while he had been a very successful debater in the House of Commons as MP for Banff and Buchan, he was unable to shine in the lesser surroundings of Holyrood.

In 2000 he resigned as leader and returned to Westminster as an ordinary MP. It was a shocking move in many ways. Here was a politician who had worked tirelessly to restore the Scottish parliament and yet he found he couldn't function in it. At least not in the way to which he was accustomed. However, while he was initially relieved to be free of the burdens of leadership, he soon became restless in obscurity. And when his party called in 2004, he accepted the leadership but only after the politician he perceived to be his main rival, Nicola Sturgeon, had withdrawn to become his deputy.

Had he planned this departure/comeback routine all in advance? Of course not. Salmond is an instinctive politician, who makes largely spontaneous judgements as much on his feel for the political moment as on extensive consultation and deliberation. This has been the secret of his success over nearly a quarter of a century as leader of the Scottish National Party. He does not get dug into entrenched positions of dogmatic principle. Take his attitude to the referendum. The "natural" position for a nationalist would, you would think, be a binary choice between independence or the Union. Yet Salmond decided in 2007, without any real opposition in the SNP, to adopt the apparently self-destructive option of placing a second constitutional choice, devolution max or quasi-federalism, on the independence ballot paper. This almost guaranteed that he would lose, since every opinion poll indicates that the Scots would vote for home rule short of full independence.

However, Salmond's strategy worked, essentially because he understood the low regard in which he was held by his political opponents. The Westminster political classes assumed that his canvassing of a third 'devo max' option in the independence referendum must be another "Nat trick". Oh no, said David Cameron, you're not having that. We're not going to allow a second best – an each way option on a two-horse race. We'll insist that if there is a referendum it should be a straight binary choice between independence and the status quo. This fractured the Scottish consensus and forced many non-nationalists into the Yes camp – around 15% – because they felt they had been effectively disenfranchised. Only around 30% of Scots have ever said they want formal independence. Yet 45% of the electorate voted to leave the United Kingdom, despite the prospect of being deprived of its currency and being excluded from the EU and NATO.

To understand the significance of the 2014 result, it is important to remember that Scotland is not an independence-minded country. Most countries seek independence because they feel they are oppressed by a foreign power, but this is simply not the case in Scotland, though some are beginning to wonder following the rough wooing on the pound. Many voters may resent the centralisation of economic, political and media life in

London, but they do not – or rather they did not – feel that they were under the imperial yoke of England. Consequently, the SNP had to argue the case for self-government in utilitarian terms of rather crude economic advantage rather than national liberation. Yet, under Salmond, they nearly made it. And he might still succeed. This game isn't over yet.

Salmond realised within hours of the defeat of the Yes campaign that the UK political establishment had left itself peculiarly vulnerable. The three party leaders had signed a solemn "vow" printed in the *Daily Record* three days before the referendum saying that Scotland would be awarded "extensive new powers" – something very close to devolution max. But no sooner had the votes been counted than the UK parties started falling out with each other. David Cameron insisted that the Scottish devolution package had to be linked to the establishment of a quasi-English parliament-within-a-parliament by introducing so-called English Votes for English laws (EVEL). This threatened the Labour leader, Ed Miliband, with the prospect of winning the next general election but finding that he was no longer in power in England over devolved matters like health, education and criminal justice. Miliband proposed instead a constitutional convention to be set up after the next UK general election to deal with English Votes for English Laws and the West Lothian Question.

Salmond saw an opportunity here to accuse the UK Government of bad faith, and perhaps even undermine the very legitimacy of the referendum result. He said that the referendum had been "trickery" and the Scottish people had been "betrayed". Scottish voters are traditionally very suspicious of the Westminster political establishment, and here it appeared as if they were not only reneging on devolution max but also turning the Scottish Question into a debate about whether or not to set up something resembling an English parliament. Salmond had correctly anticipated that he was not the best person to deal with this sense of post-referendum betrayal, however. He was damaged goods, having lost the vote. Time to pass the baton on to the next generation.

And, so, enter Nicola Sturgeon, another "queer fish" as Labourites on Twitter put it. Her election was more of a coronation than a leadership contest, since no one stood against the Deputy First Minister. This was hardy surprising – Sturgeon had effectively been leader-in-waiting since she agreed to step aside for Salmond's return in 2004 – but it didn't look very democratic. She had demonstrated an almost telepathic ability to know the mind of Alex Salmond between 2004-7 standing in for him at First Minister's Question Time in Holyrood while he was still the "absentee landlord" in Westminster. She could not be more different in temperament and style. Where Salmond is full of bonhomie and bumptiousness, she is cool, methodical – calculating even. Salmond will stay up till the small hours drinking wine with journalists, but I have never seen Nicola Sturgeon drink in their presence. She is intensely disciplined.

Since she became a nationalist while a school-girl in an Irvine comprehensive in 1986, her ideological trajectory has been rather different from that her predecessor's. Salmond might have been a member of the republican socialist '79 Group, and was even expelled from the party in 1982 for being too radical, but he always had a soft spot for bankers and latterly became almost a part of the financial establishment in Scotland. He had worked as an oil economist for RBS before entering politics, and, after 2008, he was criticised for appearing to speak too sympathetically on behalf of banks like HBOS, even as they plunged the country into chaos. He blamed "spivs and speculators" for bringing down Scottish banks, not realising that the spivs and speculators were in charge of them Sturgeon became more left wing as she matured. To use her own words, she began more as an "existential" nationalist, and evolved into a being more "utilitarian" – meaning that she now regards independence less as a thing in and of itself and more as a means to the end of social justice.

Her leftism developed while she worked as a solicitor in Drumchapel, a deprived area of Glasgow, before becoming an MSP in 1999. In the first Holyrood elections in 1999 she lost her fight in the constituency ballot for Glasgow Govan but nevertheless entered parliament because of her position on the top-up regional party list, and she later won in the redrawn constituency of Glasgow Southside. Her star rose rapidly and by 2004 she was a leadership candidate until she stood aside to let Alex Salmond return as Scottish leader after his "sabbatical" in Westminster. This established her there and then as leader in waiting. But her radicalism remained undiminished after she became a minister in 2007. One of her boasts is that, as Scottish Health Secretary, she completed the original mission of the NHS founder, the Labour minister Aneurin Bevan, when she abolished prescription charges. It is thought her policies on pensions and increasing the minimum wage would have been more radical than anything Salmond would accept in the White Paper on independence in 2013. It is also assumed that now she is in charge of the party, she will drop the proposal to cut corporation tax by 3p – a policy targeted by Labour (somewhat hypocritically, since Gordon Brown cut corporation tax when he was Chancellor). Stories emerge from time to time about Sturgeon's haggles with the intensely "prudent" Scottish Finance Secretary, John Swinney. But there has never been any hint of serious disagreement between herself and her mentor, the First Minister.

Nicola Sturgeon is a feminist but not a very militant one, and doesn't go in for gestures. She supports gender quotas on public boards, but I have never heard her complain about male domination, or glass ceilings. Sturgeon didn't initially approve of the proposal to eliminate corroboration in rape cases, as advocated by the Justice Secretary Kenny McAskill in 2012. But as the minister responsible for the Yes campaign, she ensured that the centrepiece of the independence White Paper, *Scotland's Future* (much of which she wrote herself in a frantic four weeks) was a promise of free child care which would release 100,000 women – it argued – into the workplace. A policy, it was pointed out, the achievement of which doesn't necessarily require independence. She also ensured that her party opposed the restoration of the married couples allowance.

Sturgeon is an immensely capable politician, who managed to run the Scottish health service – normally a political graveyard – for six years without a major upset, even through the swine flu pandemic in 2009. Civil servants respect her, she is well liked by colleagues, and doesn't have any of the "wide-boy side" of Alex Salmond. Her performance in the referendum campaign won plaudits, not just for her speaking style – used to devastating effect against George Galloway in the Big Big Debate at Glasgow's Hydro on the eve of the referendum – but also her television interviews.

Sturgeon manages at least to appear to answer interviewers' questions and is rarely flustered by hostile questioning.

However, Alex Salmond will enter history as Scotland's first truly national political leader, and he will be a hard act to follow. Her honeymoon with the press is short lived; tabloid style columnists have even praised her dress-sense and hair-style, though her clothes could hardly be regarded as fashionable or striking. Appearances do matter in politics, however much we pretend that they don't. Salmond's weight problems made him a figure of ridicule, the butt of cartoonists like *The Guardian*'s Steve Bell. This was something that undoubtedly affected Salmond's confidence in the later years in office – he's not nearly as thick-skinned as people think. But Sturgeon is one of those rare people who seem to become rather better-looking as they get older, as pictures of her early years in politics confirm. She wears it well, and when she took over as First Minister at 44 she looked years younger. Which is just as well because Nicola Sturgeon could be around a long time. She dislikes comparisons with the German Chancellor, Angela Merkel – not least because Merkel is a conservative – but Sturgeon has a robust political personality and an ability to appeal across gender and class barriers in much the same way. Sturgeon is the only politician in Scotland who can sell out major entertainment venues like the Glasgow Hyrdo, as she did on her post-referendum tour.

However, I doubt if this press infatuation will last. Nicola Sturgeon will soon, I suspect, be discovered to be an even worse demagogue than Alex Salmond. She is, as as Ruth Davidson, the Scottish Tory leader, has already pointed out, "the most far left First Minister in the history of the Scottish parliament", hostile to home ownership, and in the pocket of public sector trades unions. Both Conservatives and Labour believe she will alienate middle-class voters and business. She is not especially comfortable with finance and will have to sort out her views on the continuation of the Barnett Formula, which she appears sometimes to believe is essential to Scotland's economic well being and at others condemns as a Westminster "financial squeeze". Detractors in the press are already pointing out that she was not elected, even by her own party, as First Minister, but was wafted into office unopposed. The SNP under Salmond was accused, by the Labour MP Anas Sarwar, of running an "elective dictatorship" in Holyrood, but at least he had been elected. The SNP has been vulnerable to the charge of over-centralisation in government, and some in the party are concerned that the party could become a fan club for Sturgeon as it had been for Salmond, especially since she is married to the SNP's influential chief executive, Peter Murrell.

Her personality will come under intense scrutiny also. The *Daily Mail* will no doubt continue to paint her as a childless political calculating machine who doesn't understand family life, wants to abolish married couples allowance, and intends to force women to give up their children to go into work in her five-year plan. She has a sense of humour but you don't see a great deal of it in public, and she is respected in the party more than actually liked. Sturgeon used to be described as a "nippy sweetie", originally by the Govan shop steward Jamie Webster, meaning in Scottish parlance that she tended to be abrupt, sharp of tongue, and uncongenial. She is certainly not a hail-fellow-well-met like Salmond, who was always ready with a joke and a soundbite for every occasion and could win over grumpy Eurosceptic farmers in the formerly Tory constituencies of North East Scotland. Expect these characteristics to be explored more fully by the press as they take her measure.

Nicola Sturgeon may also be more willing to break Salmond's promise not to call another referendum. During the campaign, she endorsed his view that there should not be another independence ballot "for a generation", but has recently been saying that "it is the people of Scotland who should decide whether to hold such a vote, not a politician", rather missing the point that it would be a politician who would have to propose one to parliament. She insists she has "no plans" for another referendum, but as everyone knows, that is politician speak for "hell yes, we're thinking about it but daren't say so just yet".

As I explained earlier, my own view is that Sturgeon is unlikely to call another referendum in the immediate future, for the simple reason that she knows she would probably lose it. She is too shrewd to follow the excitable nationalist tribes on social media who have been urging her to declare the referendum a con, demand a revote and even declare UDI. Her number one priority will be to win the 2016 Scottish parliamentary elections and install herself as the legitimate First Minister of Scotland. Nothing will be done to undermine her prospects. The SNP membership has exploded, but it could easily implode again, and she knows how support for independence ebbs and flows. She has not ruled out any informal electoral pacts or Yes Alliance with home rule parties but she will be very cautious about diluting the SNP brand. Nicola Sturgeon is not a brilliant, inspirational politician like her predecessor, but a disciplined, focussed organiser, and she will keep her eye on the main prize. Her biggest handicap perhaps might turn out to be the extraordinary success the SNP has enjoyed since the referendum, not least in membership. She should enjoy it while she can, because it certainly won't last.

SALMOND REDUX

Nicola Sturgeon is the first Scottish National Party leader since William Wolfe in the 1960s to have become leader without having served in Westminster. Since the party has never seen membership of the UK Parliament as anything other than a means to an end, this is not a problem for her authority in Scotland. However, she takes over at a crucial moment in UK constitutional history when the focus of constitutional debate has moved, following the referendum defeat, back to Westminster where the new devolution proposals from the Smith Commission must be implemented and where the question of English Votes for English Laws has become inextricably bound up with the future of Scotland. There were fears that her lack of understanding of the dynamics of Westminster politics might be a handicap. But fortunately help was at hand.

No sooner had the media become resigned to losing Alex Salmond to golf and the boardroom, than the First Minister began dropping hints on the BBC's *Question Time* in October 2014, that he might stand as an MP. The logic was compelling. If he wanted to hold the Unionist parties' "feet to the fire", where better to do that than in Westminster itself? The party was intoxicated by the opinion polls after the referendum which suggested that the SNP could send forty or more MPs to Westminster.

In the months after his defeat, Salmond recovered much of his energy and enthusiasm for politics – he was after all only 59 when he announced his resignation as First Minister and leader. He has made absolutely clear that, whatever he chose to do in future, it would have a political dimension. Not for him the quiet afterlife in business or quangoland. Alex Salmond had come back from obscurity before and it looked as if we could be in for another final farewell tour of Westminster from the Frank Sinatra of nationalist politics. But even he could never have predicted what would happen next.

Shortly after Nicola Sturgeon had been anointed as SNP leader, and Alex Salmond made clear his intention to return to the political stage, Labour plunged into the worst of the many leadership crises which have destabilised the party since 1999. On 25th October, little more than a month since she had supposedly been a key figure in the Better Together referendum victory, the Scottish Labour leader Johann Lamont resigned in high drama, complaining that "London Labour" had treated the party as a "branch office". In an extraordinary interview in the *Daily Record*, she described Scottish Labour MPs in Westminster as "dinosaurs", claimed that Ed Miliband had delayed her plans to oppose the bedroom tax and that the UK Labour leader had even refused to meet her to discuss more powers for Holyrood. Since the Scottish leader is supposed to be fully autonomous from Labour in Westminster, following reforms introduced after Labour's crushing election defeat in 2011, these claims of London interference were extraordinarily damaging. The very term "London Labour" is Nationalist language.

Was she telling the truth, or just covering for her own deficiencies as a politician? It had been noted by journalists that, during the referendum campaign, Johann Lamont was almost invisible. It was Jim Murphy, then a UK Labour international development spokesman, and Gordon Brown, a former UK Labour Prime Minister, who had commandeered the headlines with their speaking tours. Johann Lamont could hardly have been described as a powerful or charismatic political leader and she had failed to impose her authority over the party during the row between her devolution commission and London Labour MPs over extending the powers of the parliament. Her appearances at First Minister's Questions tended to be grim- faced and she conveyed the impression of being in a permanent bad temper. "Friends" claimed that she had been stabbed in the back by her oldest political friend, the Shadow Scottish Secretary, Margaret Curran, an allegation Curran rejects.

However, two former Labour First Ministers, Jack McConnell and Henry McLeish, entered the fray on Lamont's behalf in the days after here departure. Lord McConnell said he was "very, very angry" at how Lamont had been "undermined" by her own party for years. Henry McLeish declared that the "crisis had been ten years in the making" and said that "Westminster and UK Labour don't understand Scottish politics". The former Labour finance minister Andy Kerr chipped in on 26th October on BBC Radio quipping, "If I was a dinosaur I'd be quite offended at being compared to some of these Scottish Labour MPs". Kerr even suggested that Labour had tried to "strangle" the Scottish Parliament itself – an astonishing claim from a Scottish Labour politician who was once tipped himself as a possible leadership candidate. It was a revealing insight into the state of relations within the Labour Party and indicated almost a state of internal civil war. That the Labour party in Scotland had been manipulated by its London leadership for its narrow electoral ends was a claim that had frequently been made by the SNP, but no one expected it to be confirmed quite so graphically. Labour's internal turmoil was an unexpected boost to the newly installed SNP leader Nicola Sturgeon.

THE EGG MAN ENTERS THE RACE

The candidates that emerged to replace Johann Lamont illustrated the problem faced by Labour in coming to terms with the post-referendum world. Sarah Boyack, the former environment minister, was on the feminist, green, non-confrontational wing of the party. She had been in Donald Dewar's first cabinet, and was well liked and competent, but was seen to lack the personal projection necessary to be a leader. Neil Findlay, the party's Scottish Health and Wellbeing Secretary, came from the left of the party and was an outspoken opponent of nuclear weapons. A former bricklayer-turned-teacher, he had the support of the main trades unions in Scotland like Unison. But the front runner from the start was a politician who in many ways summed up all that had gone wrong with the Labour Party since the days of Tony Blair and the Iraq war: Jim Murphy. [50]

Murphy was an outstandingly able candidate. He had taken the safest Tory seat in Scotland, Strathkelvin and Bearsden, in 1997 by sheer hard work; had gone on to become a UK cabinet minister; and had become a major figure in the referendum campaign through his "100 towns" speaking tour, on top of an Irn Bru crate. The press loved Murphy and his back-story. He had been brought up in poverty in Glasgow and had to sleep in a drawer when he was little because there was no bed for him. He was a magnetic personality and had even written a book about football. However, he also came from the unreconstructed Blairite modernising wing of the party, was a supporter of the Iraq war, and nuclear weapons, and had voted for tuition fees and the market reforms in the NHS. The SNP condemned him immediately as a right winger sent by "London Labour" to sort out the Scottish "branch office". But Murphy showed his combative style by responding that the SNP had not introduced "a single progressive policy in seven years" and promised to ditch Alex Salmond's Offensive Behaviour at Football Grounds Act.

Jim Murphy also had a reputation for being confrontational and divisive, which was fuelled by reports, only weeks after he announced his candidature that he had told the Shadow Foreign Secretary, Douglas Alexander, to "stop meddling in the Labour Party in Scotland." He was undoubtedly the strongest personality in the campaign, and more than a little arrogant – which he demonstrated on the day his candidature was launched by "apologising to the Scottish voters" for the poor performance of his predecessors. Jim Murphy was, in every way, the best and the worst candidate for the Scottish leadership.

Scottish politics were left in a very strange place by the referendum aftermath. Instead of the losers retreating into their cave to lick their wounds, here was the Scottish National Party and the other Yes campaigners going around almost performing victory laps. Meanwhile, the Better Together coalition had been plunged into disarray and internal strife. Now Labour was at war with itself over who controlled the Scottish party. It was a situation no one could possibly have forecast, and confirmed Salmond's prediction that the new political situation was "redolent with opportunities" for the Nationalists. With Alex Salmond signalling his imminent return to the front line, the Scottish National Party now had two leaders fronting a party, which had tripled its membership and dominated the opinion polls. The Scottish Labour Party had won the referendum but was now leaderless, divided, and financially distressed because of its shrinking membership. As one seasoned observer of SNP politics put it: it's a funny old world.

CHAPTER EIGHT

The Permanent Referendum – Political Activism and the End of the United Kingdom

The Unionist commentator John McTernan was not amused. Writing in *The Scotsman* a month after the referendum he complained that "the losers are strutting around like victors and the winners look like battered and bruised losers." Better Together won the 2014 referendum by a considerably greater margin than the opinion polls had forecast. It was supposed to have ended the constitutional debate for at least a generation; indeed, Westminster politicians like David Cameron and the former Cabinet Minister Jack Straw suggested that this was the matter resolved for good and all. The Scots had said, finally, that they wanted to remain in the UK. End of. Except it wasn't. The defeated independence campaign went through a spasm of grief and then carried on as if nothing had happened. In the weeks and months following the referendum there were rolling demonstrations and events almost by the week involving thousands of people under banners like Voice of the People, Hope over Fear, Women for Independence, Radical Independence. This infuriated the Unionists of Better Together who had been insisting that the losers should "get over it" and "move on".

Normally, the losing forces in an election undergo a period of introspection and consolidation. But not this time. The membership of the Scottish National Party more than trebled in the two months following the referendum to 84,000 making the SNP the third largest party in the United Kingdom after Labour. Indeed, scaled up, this would be equivalent to a UK party membership of over 800,000. The Scottish Green Party's membership quadrupled to more than 7,000 and the Scottish Socialist Party also had a comparable increase in numbers. Labour's Scottish membership meanwhile remained at a claimed 13,000. The SNP became the fastest growing political party in Europe after the left wing Spanish party Podemos (We Can). Local SNP groups found that instead of tens turning up to their constituency meetings, they were attracting hundreds. This is the kind of afterglow that normally accompanies a great election victory – like Labour's general election landslide in 1997 – not a crushing defeat.

On 30th October 2014, an Ipsos/Mori opinion poll for STV put the SNP support in voting intentions for Westminster at an astonishing 52% – 29 points ahead of Labour.[51] Had this been reflected in any general election, it would have given the SNP 54 seats to Labour's 4. Yet as recently as 2010, Labour had returned 41 out of 59 Scottish seats, and the SNP only 6. *The Spectator* blogger Alex Massie described it as "the most astonishing survey of Scottish political opinion in living memory". The very next day, another slightly less sensational opinion poll from YouGov put the SNP 'only' 16% ahead of Labour for Westminster and suggested that, had there been a general election the next day, the SNP would have returned with 47 seats, and possibly held the balance of power in the UK parliament. It was becoming clear that while Westminster had won the referendum, it was losing Scotland.

Nationalists on the internet started speculating about Alex Salmond becoming deputy Prime Minister of the UK in the way Nick Clegg had after the 2010 bargaining between the Liberal Democrats and the Conservatives. This was always fantasy politics, of course, because the SNP do not vote on English issues in Westminster, observing their own version of English Votes for English Laws. That alone would rule out Alex Salmond or any SNP Westminster leader joining a UK cabinet. Nevertheless, the idea that the SNP could become king-makers – in the way the Bloc Quebecois had in the Canadian federal parliament in the early 1990s – was tantalising. Of course, these opinion polls occurred shortly after the Labour leadership crisis and no one, even in the independence movement, believed that this level of popularity could last. However, as Labour struggled to cope with its internal contradictions following Johann Lamont's resignation as leader on 25th October 2014, it seemed as if its grip on Scotland could finally be disintegrating.

This was all bizarrely counter-intuitive. Why would Scottish voters turn in such numbers to a party after they had just rejected the policy on which it based its entire politics? The referendum campaign had been running for two and a half years, so it was not as if the Scottish voters had been forced to make a decision in haste. More than 2 million Scots had voted to remain in the United Kingdom, more than half the adult population. Why would large numbers of them subsequently decide that they had made the wrong choice? Of course, voting SNP has never been quite the same as voting for independence. Scots elected Alex Salmond on a landslide in 2011 not because they wanted to leave the UK but because they regarded the Scottish National Party as by far the best party to run the devolved Scottish Parliament. But this seemed to be something more than just an expression of instrumental support for the SNP as the best team for Holyrood.

The Scots appeared genuinely to be having second thoughts about the way they had voted in September 2014. Why else would no fewer than two thirds have told the Ipsos/Mori pollsters in their poll on 31st October that they were willing to see another referendum within ten years?[52] Perhaps even more surprising was that, in the same opinion poll, more than half said they would be happy with another referendum within five years. 55% said there should be a referendum on independence if the UK voted to leave the EU in the proposed in/out referendum in 2017. This wasn't just a few nationalist diehards on the internet calling for a revote; it suggested that there was widespread discontent in Scotland about how the UK parties had conducted themselves since the referendum. So, what was it that got Scotland's goat?

The attempt by David Cameron to tie English Votes for English Laws (EVEL) to future devolution to Scotland did not go down well. "Just as the people of Scotland will have more powers over their own affairs" he declared at 7am on the morning after the referendum, "so it follows that the people of England, Wales and Northern Ireland must have a bigger say over theirs." Perhaps, but there had been no indication in any of the speeches and declarations of Better Together that the search for further devolution for Scotland had to go "in tandem", as the PM put it, with fundamental constitutional change south of the Border. In fact, opinion polls indicated that by a considerable majority Scots supported the idea of EVEL, but that wasn't the point. In the weeks immediately after the referendum, Scotland was largely forgotten as the UK media went on to explore the implications, mostly negative in the case of Labour Party leader Ed Miliband, of the establishment of a defacto devolved English Parliament in Westminster. This coincided with the rejection of "devolution max" by the Unionist parties on the Smith Commission, which had been convened to deliver on the three party "Vow" of extensive new powers for Holyrood. Many Scots clearly believed that the extensive new powers promised by Gordon Brown would be something more than just the sum of the partial proposals from the Unionist parties in the Better Together campaign.

Nor was affection for the Union enhanced by the spectacle of the Scottish Labour leader, Johann Lamont, resigning on the grounds that "London Labour" had been making her life impossible by bossing the Scottish party around. The talk of Westminster "dinosaurs" and the revelation that many of her predecessors as Scottish Labour leader had similarly felt under the leash of London was extremely damaging in Scotland which has traditionally been a Labour-supporting country, at least in Westminster elections. If Lamont had resigned a month before the referendum instead of a month after it, Scotland would probably have been an independent country by now. It really was that close.

The whole post-referendum period read like one of the paranoid, internet nationalist fantasies about life after a No vote. A new oil field was discovered in the North Sea, apparently confirming the theory that the UK had been concealing the true extent of oil wealth. The headline in *The Times* on 23rd September – 'Cameron to cut public funds for Scotland' – seemed to confirm fears that the Barnett Formula for Scottish spending was under threat. The London Mayor led a chorus of English Tory MPs saying that spending promises given to Scots were "reckless" and that Scotland could no "longer expect to get £1,500 more per head" spending than the UK average. Social justice had been a prominent theme in the referendum campaign, so it struck a sour note when, at the Conservative Party conference in October, the Chancellor, George Osborne, announced a tax giveaway to the relatively wealthy on inheritance tax while cutting benefits in real terms to the unemployed and working poor. The UK media became even more infatuated with Nigel Farage as UKIP gained its first ever MP in the Clacton-on-Sea by-election. BBC election planners ruled that UKIP, with one Westminster seat, would participate in the leadership debates in the May general election, whereas the Scottish National Party with six and the Green Party with one, would not. In awe of UKIP's advance, David Cameron ramped up his rhetoric against the European Union, demanding an end to the free movement of labour and signalled his government's intention to repeal the Human Rights Act. He seemed unaware that the European Convention on Human Rights is already written into the Scotland Act.

Throughout the referendum campaign, Better Together had repeatedly claimed that voting for independence would jeopardise Scotland's continued membership of the European

Union. But after the referendum, it became clear that Scotland, by remaining in the UK, had placed itself at risk of being taken out of Europe by the proposed in-out referendum in 2017. It has long been the case that Scots are more favourable to remaining in the European Union than voters in England. In November 2014, YouGov confirmed that 57% of Scots would vote to stay in the EU in any future referendum against 37% across the UK as a whole. Just 28% said they would vote to leave against 47% in the UK.[53] Nicola Sturgeon, newly installed as SNP leader, infuriated many in Westminster when she called for Scotland to have an effective veto on any Brexit vote in the proposed 2017 referendum.

Her argument was that in federal systems, like Canada, provincial governments have a right to be consulted on existential issues such as this. She argued that in the "family of nations" that make up the United Kingdom, all members should agree before the household decides to move out of Europe. The idea of a regional veto was batted away by David Cameron at Prime Minister's Question Time and ridiculed in the press. "What part of No does Nicola Sturgeon not understand?" demanded the UKIP MEP David Coburn on BBC radio. "Will Nicola Sturgeon turnout to be as annoying as Alex Salmond was?" asked the *Daily Telegraph. The Scotsman* accused her of "behaving as if she were First Minister of a fully federal state" and reminded her that Scotland had just voted to remain in the UK.

These reactions made absolutely clear to any Scottish voters who still believed that they were about to get "devolution max", that the UK remained very much a unitary state with Westminster in control. Indeed, the SNP raised the veto to demonstrate this. It also confirmed Scotland would have no choice but to leave the EU if the UK voted for Brexit. Nicola Sturgeon also wanted to raise the constitutional anomaly implied by the Northern Ireland Act 1998. A product of the Good Friday Agreement, this legislation gives the people of Northern Ireland the sovereign right to decide their own future and to leave the UK if they aren't happy with Westminster rule.[54] The province therefore has essentially what Nicola Sturgeon was calling for: the right to hold its own referendum on membership of the EU. The difference, however, is that Northern Ireland could opt to join the Irish Republic, whereas Scotland has no such escape route.

All this contributed to the general impression of "business as usual" for the UK after the referendum. Nationalists had always predicted that Scotland would cease to figure in Westminster after a No vote – as happened after the abortive devolution referendum in 1979. Nothing that happened in the months immediately following the referendum served to confound their pessimism. It may also be that the Scots were reflecting on the way they had, as many saw it, been coerced into voting No by the three UK parties ganging up to deny an independent Scotland access to the pound. The knowledge that the Labour leader, Ed Miliband, had promised to put in Labour's election manifesto that Scots would never be allowed to use the pound, rankled. Many working-class Scots never forgave Labour for sharing a platform with the Conservatives in Better Together in the first place. Opinion polls indicated that even No voters had rejected the UK's claims to sole possession of the currency of the UK, and as I indicated in chapter Two, many Scots regarded this as rough wooing. The experience of the referendum underlined to many the importance of ensuring that they elected political parties that promoted Scottish interests within the Union. The most obvious candidate to do this was, of course, the Scottish National Party. Labour seemed no longer able or willing to articulate Scotland's interests.

Labour used to describe itself as "Scotland's national party" and with some justification. Scottish voters kept faith with Labour through its darkest years in the 1980s when it was all but unelectable in the South of England. One reason why Tony Blair's cabinets had so many Scots – Robin Cook, Gordon Brown, Alistair Darling, George Robertson etc. – was because Scotland still sent MPs in large numbers to Westminster – over 50 in 1987 – nearly a quarter of the entire UK Parliamentary Labour Party. However, Scotland has not always been Labour territory. Indeed, as recently as the 1950s, it was the Scottish Unionists who dominated parliamentary elections, and in 1955 the SUP returned a majority of votes and seats – something no party has succeeded in emulating, though given the drift of the opinion polls, the Scottish National Party might just break that record.

The Scottish Unionists became the Conservative and Unionist party in 1965, but it was never really a Tory party. In fact, that name change proved to be an unmitigated disaster and led to the virtual extinction of the party in Scotland. The Scottish Unionists had emerged out of the wreckage of the old Liberal Party in 1912 after it split over Irish Home Rule and were never similar to the Conservative Party in England. The SUP was a distinctively

Scottish party and promoted some very un-Tory things like social housing in the 1930s. It may be that some of the dormant DNA of the old Unionist party have now recombined in the Scottish National Party. The SNP is not only more left wing than the Labour Party, it is more Scottish and more liberal. It is possible that Labour's dominance in Scotland, so complete in the 1980s, may only have been a transitory phenomenon. Now that Scotland has started to re-examine its place in the United Kingdom, it may be that Labour will be eclipsed just as the old Scottish Unionists were eclipsed before them.

The heretical thought began to occur privately to some nationalists that, from a purely party political point of view, it may actually have been in the SNP's interest to lose the referendum, so long as it came a good second. Had Scotland actually voted for independence on the ill-formed currency prospectus of the Yes campaign, and given the belligerent attitude of the Westminster parties, there would almost certainly have been a financial crisis. The flight of funds had already begun before September 18th. The autumn of 2014 saw the biggest capital outflow from the UK since the collapse of Lehman Brothers in 2008. Of course, this was largely a consequence of the refusal by the Westminster parties to contemplate any currency union which was designed to create a climate of financial instability in Scotland. Nevertheless, voters dislike instability wherever it comes from and the turmoil might have turned voters against the sitting government in Scotland – the Scottish National Party.

During complex negotiations over Europe, defence, welfare, and with the prospect of cuts in public spending to build up currency reserves, it is quite possible that the Scots love affair with nationalism might have soured. Indeed, had Scotland actually voted Yes, Scottish voters might have installed Labour, or a Lib-Lab coalition, as the first government of an independent Scotland. Moreover, the alliance of convenience between the fundamentalist wing of the Scottish National Party, as represented by Gordon Wilson, and the gradualist/federalists, might have come under intolerable strain. This is all in the realms of speculation of course, and we can all play "what might have been". The important thing is that, for whatever reason, the parties that lost the referendum emerged from the campaign vastly more powerful than when they went in.

INDEPENDENCE POSTPONED

Somehow, in the crucible of the referendum campaign, a fundamental shift appears to have taken place in Scottish attitudes to independence. So, what was the nature of this change, and how enduring might it be? Before the SNP's opinion poll surge in late October, *The Guardian* commentator Martin Kettle wrote a provocative piece comparing the aftermath of the referendum to the Irish Easter Rising in 1916.

> No one who spent time in Scotland during the referendum campaign was in any doubt that they were witnessing something new. Partly, this sense of a generational break was magnified by the strength of pro-independence feeling on social media, all of which tended to reflect itself to itself with ever growing excitement. But the sense of a gathering generational rejection of past Scottish politics was palpable. And the defeat of independence seems barely to have slowed it. The sometimes malign incompetence of the victors may have fuelled it even more. (22/10/14)

Kettle made clear, of course, that he did not expect this generational change to be as bloody as had been the case in Ireland, and he perhaps overestimates the revolutionary potential of the Scottish people. Nevertheless, there are many people who had direct experience of the referendum campaign who came to the same conclusion. The writer Adam Ramsay put it this way in *Open Democracy*:

> This flood of new activists still yearns for that fairer society. They are still willing to trudge the streets and mobilise their friends and stand up to the powerful to demand it. They have learned what it is like to think big and to believe that radical change is possible. And once people realise that their dreams can't be contained in a 30-second TV ad, once they have tasted a smidgeon of their own power to win those dreams, they never go back. (15/10/14)

Some observers, including the Channel 4 journalist Paul Mason, had mused on the comparisons between the 2014 referendum and popular movements like Occupy and the Arab Spring. Others have drawn parallels with the civic nationalist movements that overthrew communism in Eastern Europe after the fall of the Berlin Wall. These comparisons are of course largely specious. The UK is not a dictatorship or a communist totalitarian regime, and people in Scotland have full civil rights. However, there were some echoes of previous forms of civic dissent. The involvement in the Yes campaign of many young and working-class activists using social media to organise, was in some ways similar to the recent mass democratic street campaigns from Occupy to Tahrir Square. Twitter and Facebook became alternative news agencies, projecting a very different message from that in the mainstream media. And like the Velvet Revolutions in Eastern Europe, Scotland's nationalist movement was non-sectarian, peaceful, and rigorously democratic. It was also strongly influenced by artists and writers in groups like National Collective. Uniquely for a mass political movement of this scale and demographic there was no hint of real violence. The extreme anti-capitalist and anarchist groups that exploited demonstrations like Make Poverty History in 2005 and the student demonstration against tuition fees in 2010, setting fire to Parliament Square, were almost completely absent. The Scottish uprising policed itself with a spontaneous discipline and prevented either agent provocateurs or militant extremists from using their movement as a stage for violent confrontation.

Of course, people do lose interest eventually. It happened to the Occupy movement, for example, which appeared to be such a vigorous campaign in 2011, but disappeared almost as quickly as it had emerged. It happened also, with more disastrous results, to the Arab Spring. It is hard to live life for very long at this level of political intensity. However, it looked as if the infrastructure might now be in place in Scotland to maintain, if not this extraordinary level of political engagement we saw during the referendum campaign, then at least a long-term campaign to win self-government. There has certainly never been an independence movement on this scale in Scotland before, and I don't just mean here the extraordinary inflation of the SNP's membership. There emerged from the referendum an array of organisations, overlapping but distinct, which grew out of the official Yes campaign but which now had resources, membership, high morale and a determination to keep on pressing for constitutional change. They refused to accept defeat and many had started organising for the next referendum.

Some 100,000 people, according to the SNP chief executive Peter Murrell, were actively involved in the Yes campaign in one way or another. They were recruited by the various Yes campaigns that were formed by Yes Scotland to take the message to specific sectors, like Business for Scotland, Women for Independence, Generation Yes, Asians for Yes, Radical Independence Campaign etc. These groups not only continued in existence after the official Yes Scotland campaign folded on 19th September – they have in most cases grown rapidly and there were moves to keep them all together in a Yes Alliance. There are in addition around 300 street corner Yes supporting groups, many of which refused to disband after the referendum. They are joined by other organisations like Common Weal, the Green Party, the Scottish Socialists and a range of internet-based bodies like Bella Caledonia and National Collective. It is not easy to say exactly how many people these organisations represent, but collectively they clearly speak for a significant proportion of the 1.6 million Scots who voted Yes. Largely mobilised through social media, having lost trust in the mainstream media, they represent a new departure in radical politics in Britain.

This multiplicity of Yes-oriented political groups undoubtedly helped the SNP to widen its appeal beyond traditional nationalists, and allowed the independence campaign to continue as a going concern despite the referendum defeat. This is a movement now with a very large following, a decentralised organisation and its own channels of communication. Both Common Weal and Bella Caledonia have attempted to set up alternative news agencies to by-pass the conventional media. These groups cannot be dismissed merely as shop-windows for the Scottish National Party, and many have significant disagreements with the SNP on policy issues like top rate taxation, an independent currency and support for the monarchy. However, though they have diverse ideologies, all of these groups recognise the right of the Scottish National Party, with its greatly expanded membership, to lead the campaign for independence. This nationalist movement is now the driving force in Scottish politics.

It may be of course that, given the sheer diversity of groups involved, and the presence of the far left with its proclivity for factionalism, that this movement may end up arguing with itself and losing public support. Already some of the language being used by the more extreme elements on social media has caused problems. The reality is that the Nationalists will need to win over middle-class voters and ex-Labour party supporters who are not impressed by language such as this from Alan McGee, the head of Creation Records, on the eve of the Hope over Fear demonstration: "Westminster careerists and the bitches of big business and the whores of warmongers don't even blush [*sic*] over as they mutter trite mea culpas for their failures".[55]

On the whole however the broad Scottish independence movement has been remarkably disciplined given its lack of any central organisation. Indeed, that lack of any kind of top-down organisation is probably one of its strengths. The virtue of nationalism as a political ideology is that it allows groups with different ideologies and programmes to work together for a common end. There is no doubt that working in the Yes campaign was a transformative experience for many of the political activists involved in it, particularly those parties from the far left. They discovered that together they were more than the sum of their parts. The huge response from the people of Scotland overwhelmed their inbuilt proclivity to sectarianism.

There are many disagreements within the movement about how exactly to proceed. As I have explained in earlier chapters, amorphous groups like The 45 claim the referendum is rigged and want to find an alternative road to independence, perhaps including direct action. But most accept the reality of the referendum result and see the future as some form of federalism. A new home rule group inspired by the Conservative-leaning think tank, Reform, was launched in November 2014 by the former Labour First Minister Henry McLeish and the former SNP MSP Andrew Wilson. At the other end of the spectrum is the Independence Convention, a cross party group established a decade ago by a number of nationalists around the actress Elaine C Smith, to widen support for independence. They hope to capitalise on the referendum experience by turning the continuing Yes campaign into a broad Home Rule movement. It was felt that, if the SNP simply took over the remnants of the Yes campaign, many of the people who had become involved who were not natural nationalists would be alienated.

It is impossible to tell how all this will develop. But it seems likely that, whatever happens, this broad independence movement will continue to define Scottish politics for the foreseeable future. Indeed, it is difficult to see what can be done at UK level to undermine it. Scotland has, over many decades, developed a more social democratic political culture than exists certainly in the south of England. Westminster politics has been going in a different direction on a whole range of issues from Europe to welfare policy, immigration, the renewal of Trident, tuition fees, to marketisation of public services. There has been no sign of any Conservative revival in Scotland, and the Labour party has been caught in the contradiction of seeking to win votes in the south while trying to appease its Scottish supporters. With the decline of industrial class politics, and the rise of regionalism in Europe, nationalism is proving to be a new organising principle of democratic engagement. The old left's suspicion of nationalism is not shared by young people who increasingly see independence as the only viable challenge to globalisation and the dominance of neoliberalism. The apparent success of the Nordic model in providing a social democratic escape route from globalisation has revived faith in radical action, in the possibility of creating "a better nation" as nationalists invariably put it.

None of this was inevitable. It is important to remember that Scotland was a very firm part of the United Kingdom until very recently. It is really only in the last decade that large numbers of Scots have started to think seriously about independence as a practical possibility. This is one reason why the Scottish Nationalists had such difficulty with issues like the currency. Scottish voters were not used to thinking about the mechanics of setting up an independent state, and this all created a great sense of anxiety. But nationalists are in this for the long game and they have made extraordinary progress in the last year by persuading 45% of Scottish voters to back independence. It seems highly likely that there will be demand for another referendum on independence. It may not come for another generation, but fifteen or twenty years is, for supporters of independence, not a long time to wait. I have seen extraordinary changes in Scottish attitudes to self-government in the past twenty years that I would never have believed possible. The hundreds of thousands of Scots who have been persuaded that they need independence to create a fairer nuclear free society – they are not going to go away. It is my firm belief now, having seen the reaction to the referendum, that Scotland will be an independent country. And we may not have to wait very long to see it.

ACKNOWLEDGEMENTS

This book is based on countless conversations with politicians and non-politicians. I am immensely grateful to my editor Mark Buckland of Cargo for pulling it all together in six weeks. Also help and insights from Simon Cree, Tom Devine, Noel Dolan, Rob Edwards, Jonathan Freedland, Susan Flockhart, Peter Geoghegan, David Greig, Gerry Hassan, Stewart Kirkpatrick, James Maxwell, Ewen MacAskill, Nicola McEwen, James Robertson, Tommy Sheppard, Sarah Beattie Smith, Gill Tasker, Ben Thompson, Adam Tompkins, David Torrance and Richard Walker.

All the views expressed are my own not theirs, and so are all the mistakes.

The publisher would like to thank Dr Scott Lyall.

REFERENCES

1 'Scottish independence referendum: 'The old union is dead', warns First Minister Carwyn Jones', Wales Online, http://bit.ly/1wXuzDJ

2 'Scotland started a glorious revolution. Don't let Westminster snuff it out', The Guardian, http://bit.ly/1uvgHlQ

3 'Yes Scotland sheds more senior staff as funding doubts reemerge', The Guardian, http://bit.ly/1Hke2Ci

4 'Lottery winners Colin and Chris Weir donate 79% of Yes Scotland funds', The Guardian, http://bit.ly/1EZET2w

5 'Scottish independence: poll reveals who voted, how and why', The Guardian, http://bit.ly/1xCysmR

6 'Alex Salmond must leave Alistair Darling 'on the floor' in independence TV debate', The Telegraph, http://bit.ly/1uPXsF7

7 A Mensah, 'The Process of Monetary Decolonisation in Africa', UTAFITI: Journal of the Arts and Social Sciences, Volume 1, July, 1979, p. 4, http://bit.ly/1F2SIPD

8 'A currency union would be best for all of Britain', Financial Times, http://on.ft.com/1xohszv

9 'Independent Scotland 'may keep pound' to ensure stability', The Guardian, http://bit.ly/1tdX91J

10 'Investors pull massive £16.6bn out of the UK for fear of Scotland exit in biggest flight of capital since Lehman crisis', This Is Money, http://bit.ly/1BMyHhT

11 'Scottish independence: currency union 'incompatible with sovereignty', The Guardian, http://bit.ly/1uPXsF7

12 'Carney: massive shortfall in currency reserves for independent Scotland', The Guardian, http://bit.ly/1uazQpw

13 'Scottish independence: currency union 'incompatible with sovereignty', The Guardian, http://bit.ly/1uPXsF7

14 Fears more firms will follow Standard Life threat to quit, The Herald, http://bit.ly/1gIPuDM

15 'Scotland ahead of rUK even without oil says Credit Suisse report', Newsnet Scotland, http://bit.ly/1voX4PY

16 'Scots believe Osborne is 'bluffing' over currency', The Times, http://thetim.es/1rEyOVm

17 'YouGov Report Dramatic Swing to Yes', What Scotland Thinks, http://bit.ly/1uPZ8ya

18 'Hope Over Fear Rally: Thousands gather in George Square for pro-independence demonstration', The Daily Record, http://bit.ly/1uvjpYF

19 'I want fewer walls and barriers and to be wonderfully, quirkily British', The Guardian, http://bit.ly/1q36yqV

20 'BBC Propaganda Hits New All-Time Low', Craig Murray, http://bit.ly/1uvjDik

21 'Are Scottish artists too afraid to say No?', The Telegraph, http://bit.ly/1uvjITl

22 The Scotsman, http://bit.ly/1xCA6Fb

23 'Scottish independence would have a devastating impact on the BBC', The Guardian, http://bit.ly/1zCKY3O

24 'The No camp is losing out in this carnival of democracy', The Herald, http://bit.ly/1AGL5My

25 'SNP steps up its borrowing despite big donations', The Herald, http://bit.ly/1ySi2nx

26 'Bought and sold or hype in bold: Newspaper framing of the Scottish independence debate', http://bit.ly/1voY1Yy

27 'Think-tank: Scotland's economy stronger than previously thought', Business For Scotland, http://bit.ly/14KNFGO

28 Twitter @BritNatAbuse 1) http://bit.ly/1BMBdom 2) http://bit.ly/1ynQu9w 3) http://bit.ly/14KPZ0c 4) http://bit.ly/1qWf7WD

29 'Fears of disorder as Yes surges to record high in referendum poll', Politics, http://bit.ly/1BMCvzU

30 'Police Federation dismiss reports of referendum campaign disorder', STV, http://bit.ly/1zCMp26

31 'Survey reveals voters turn to newspapers for information on Scottish Independence', Press Gazette, http://bit.ly/1sVqvpT

32 Bella Caledonia, http://bit.ly/1p1tPzJ

33 John Robertson, 'Fairness In the First Year? BBC and ITV Coverage of the Scottish referendum campaign from September 2012 to September 2013', Issuu, http://bit.ly/1p1nV1J

34 'Treasury briefed RBS move before board decision', BBC, http://bbc.in/1zCMLWH

35 'Retailers under pressure to back no vote in Scottish referendum', The Guardian, http://bit.ly/1qqTWkP

36 'Balance failure in BBC Scottish independence referendum coverage 'wrong and not acceptable' says Channel 4's Stuart Cosgrove', The Drum, http://bit.ly/1xPNeo2

37 'SNP wanted a Nazi Invasion', Scottish Research Society 13/9/14, http://bit.ly/1AhUSLk

38 'Lord George Robertson: Forces of Darkness Would Love Scottish Split from United Kingdom', Brookings, http://brook.gs/1xUuNzp

39 'Why has fascism entered the indy ref?', Scottish Review, http://bit.ly/1xot99v

40 'The Caledonian Antisyzygy and the Gaelic Ideal', in *Selected Essays of Hugh MacDiarmid*, ed. Duncan Glen, 1969, p.70.

41 George Orwell, 'Notes on Nationalism', http://bit.ly/1bf61w2

42 Tom Nairn, The Break-Up of Britain, 1977; 1978 p. 348.

43 'Why the left is wrong about immigration', The Guardian, http://bit.ly/1xPBLom

44 'SNP submission to Smith Commission', SNP, http://bit.ly/1xP7qX7

45 'Federalism and Economic Reform: International Perspectives' by Jessica Wallack and T. N. Srinivasan, 2006, p. 200.

46 'The Day After Judgement', Policy Scotland, http://bit.ly/1p1os3y

47 'Poll: how Alex Salmond splits voter opinion', The Herald, http://bit.ly/1qqVMCf

48 'Ipsos MORI latest Scottish Public Opinion Monitor', Scotland Votes, http://bit.ly/1F2ZxAI

49 'Scottish Independence Referendum: Salmond described as 'arrogant, ambitious and dishonest' by Scottish women', Independent, http://ind.pn/1qqWbo8

50 Scots Labour front runner Jim Murphy fuels campaign 'flop' storm, Daily Mail, http://dailym.ai/1xCE1C0

51 'STV poll: SNP at 52% as Labour face general election meltdown', STV, http://bit.ly/1qWiZGS

52 'Scottish independence: 66% back new referendum', The Scotsman, http://bit.ly/1F3031A

53 'Scots want to stay in the EU as the rest of Britain wants to say goodbye', The Herald, http://bit.ly/1vpybDc

54 'British withdrawal from the EU: an existential threat to the United Kingdom?', Future UK and Scotland, http://bit.ly/1vp1Bli

55 'Scottish Independence Is Coming - It's Not If It's When!', Huffington Post, http://huff.to/1p1oTel

APPENDICES

Appendice One: Leading stories in the Referendum Campaign as compiled by Press Data's Referendum Daily, 1/9/2014 – 17/9/2014

1/9/14
TOP: "Think tank puts iScotland set-up costs at over £2bn" (CEBR) *NO*
"Salmond: referendum debate 'most empowering in Scottish history' " (On basis of huge increase in those registering to vote) *YES*
"Police to be stationed at polling stations as safeguard against tensions" (Quoting Mary Pitcaithly, Chief Counting Officer) *NO*
"SNP planning for 'lame duck' government: reports civil service source" *NO*
OTHER: "Farage to visit Glasgow" *NEUTRAL*
"Academics fear Brain Drain" (Universities are bracing themselves for an exodus of some of their leading scientists after a Yes vote) *NO*

2/9
TOP: "New poll shows gap narrowing" *YES*
"Better Together reveal new poster campaign" (appeals to Parents) *NO*
"Police concerned over 'referendum security matters'" (Murphy egging) *NO*
"Former PM says Scotland will be "outcast" Brown speech *NO*
OTHER: "SNP ministers deny relaunch post No vote" (report that civil servants been called on to relaunch SNP government) *NO*
"Yes vote will give LGBT community greater equality" *YES*
"Facebook could swing vote" NEUTRAL

3/9
TOP: "Pro-Union insider: Independence a real possibility" *YES*
"EU membership incompatible with 'sterlingisation' claim" (Oli Rehn ex-EU commission) *NO*
"Jim Murphy resumes referendum tour" (more allegations of disruption by Yes) *NO*
OTHER:"Ex ambassadors: Nato will welcome Scotland" *YES*
"Mountaineers seek answers on wild land" *NEUTRAL*

4/9
 TOP: "Union best for social justice, Miliband to say" *NO*
"Warnings for sterling stability with indy" (Goldman Sachs predict euro-zone currency crisis) *NO*
"Concerns expressed over 'Yes' vote by CBI head" *NO*
OTHER: "Former Head of GCHQ expresses security concern" (Sir David Oman says SNP security and intelligence plans are seriously flawed) *NO*

"Sturgeon: Indyref mirrors 2011 victory" *YES*
"Penalty shoot out between both sides of campaign" (5/4 to Union, a pretty accurate indyref result!) *NEUTRAL*

5/9
TOP: "Ed Miliband's trip to Scotland scrutinised" NEUTRAL
"Cameron insists he won't quit if Scots vote Yes" *NO*
"Alex Salmond guest edits Daily Record" *YES*
"RMT Union backs a Yes" *YES*
"Debates over oil and gas continue" NEUTRAL
"Property and finance fears over referendum" *NO*
OTHER: "Murphy egg thrower given community service" (Stuart McKenzie 80 days unpaid community service) *NO*
"Bismark hero says yes vote a betrayal" *NO*
"Geldof appeals for a No vote" *NO*
"Frankie Boyle to host referendum TV show" *NEUTRAL*

6/9
TOP: "Labour to bring 100 MPs to fight for the Union" *NO*
"Nato membership for an indy Scotland questioned" *NO*
OTHER: "Football legends sign up for Better Together" *NO*
"JK Rowling attacks SNP over scaremongering" *NO*
"Referendum a threat to marriage, warns counsellor" (Relationships Scotland chief executive says "different views on independence may drive couples apart") *NO*

7/9
TOP: "Shock new poll places Yes ahead for the first time 51-49%" *YES*
"JK Rowling calls for calm" ('People before flags, answers not slogans, reason not ranting', she tweeted) *NO*
"Unionist parties 'to agree terms for more devolution'" *NO*
"'Guards on the border' Warns Ed Miliband" *NO*
OTHER: "MP bemoans lack of imagination" (Tory MP Rory Stewart criticises No campaign) *YES*

8/9 **TOP:** "Unionists accused of "panic" as George Osborne promises more powers" *YES*
"Queen's concern over Yes vote" *NO*
"Yes surge will rock money markets" *NO*
OTHER: "The science of Yes – behavioural researchers at Edin Uni say more people are informed the more likely to yes" *YES*
"£350m development under threat from Yes" (GW redevelopment scheme) *NO*

9/9
TOP: "Brown leads final Labour pro-Union campaign" *NO*

"Polls lead to market tremors Standard Life, RBS Lloyds shares fall" *NO*
"Polls predict photo finish" *NEUTRAL*
OTHER: "Royal Baby 'will help unite Britain'" *NO*
"Final Darling – Salmond debate on Mumsnet) *NEUTRAL*
"Independence threatens eggs" *NO*
(Scotland's largest egg producer, farmer John Campbell of Glenrath, Peebles, throws his weight behind Better Together)

10/9
TOP: "Cameron, Miliband, and Clegg come to Scotland" (offering more powers for Scots) *NO*
"Carney: Currency union 'incompatible with sovereignty'" *NO*
"Queen to stay out of the indyref" *NEUTRAL*
"Claims money leaving Scotland with vote approaching" (Multrees Investor wealth manager service say hundreds of millions leaving : Japanese bank Nomur a predicts "cataclysmic shock" and collapse of pound) *NO*
OTHER: "Kissinger supports union" *NO*
"Brown to Focus on NHS – likens SNP to Trojan Horse" *NO*

11/9
TOP: "Westminster leaders come to Scotland" (promising more powers) *NO*
"RBS Lloyds would move HQs with Yes vote" *NO*
"Latest poll boost for *NO*" (53/47) *NO*
OTHER: "Governor opines on pound" (Carney says iScotland would need "billions in reserves" if used pound unilaterally with no currency union) *NO*
"FT and Scotsman support union" *NO*
"Academics vote *NO*" (poll in Times Higher Education Supplement) *NO*

12/9
TOP: "New YouGov poll puts Better Together back in front" *NO*
"Business 'onslaught' as 90% said to be opposed to 'Yes' vote" *NO*
"Shoppers warned of higher prices after split" (John Lewis, Asda et al.) *NO*
"Brown: Ill fight Salmond – hints he'll stand as MSP" *NO*
OTHER: "North Korea Votes Yes" (Kim Jong-Un supports indy) *NO*
"Dust up in Buchanan St" *NEUTRAL*

13/9
TOP: "Poll: No leads by two going into final week" *NO*
"Economic concerns over indy raised" (Crossborder Capital says 17bn leaving UK because of uncertainty over pound) *NO*
Buinesses face 'day of reckoning', says Sillars" (Seen as threat) *NO*
OTHER: "Farage calls for Queen to intervene" *NO*

"English voters want to stay together" *NO*

4/9

TOP: "Polls put both sides ahead" *YES*

"Thousands turn out for Orange Order and pro-independence marches" *YES*

"Salmond and Sillars split on 'Day of Reckoning'"*NO*

OTHER: "Salmond accuses BBC of Bias" *YES*

"UKIP: "Yes vote may not mean independence" *NEUTRAL*

"Oil expert votes Yes" (Alex Russell Prof of Petroleum Accounting at Robert Gordon University Aberdeen) *YES*

"Groundskeeper Willie votes Aye" (Simpsons Springfield elementary janitor supports Yes) *YES*

15/9

TOP: "Queen asks that voters "think carefully"" *NO*

"BBC subject of 'bias' protests" (Protest at Pacific Quay over Nick Robinson Alastair Campbell says: "Vote Yes for intimidation") *NO*

"Economic debate intensifies: FT runs series of articles on falling business confidence and plans of companies to leave Scotland" *NO*

"Salmond says Referendum is "Once in a Generation" opportunity" *YES*

OTHER: "Cameron: up to Scots to save UK" *NO*

"Talks on EU membership have commenced" NEUTRAL

"Beckham backs union" *NO*

16/9

TOP: "PM would be 'heartbroken' by 'Yes' vote" *NO*

"Cameron, Clegg and Miliband: More powers if Scots vote no" (Record Vow) *NO*

"Economic and business questions raised" (extra banknotes being sent to Scotland) *NO*

"'Serious' businesses see opportunities of indy, says Salmond" *YES*

OTHER: "18 Veterans criticise Lord Dannatt"(said British soldiers died in vain) *YES*

17/9

TOP: "Final day of campaigning" *NEUTRAL*

"New polls: No – 52% Yes – 48%" *NEUTRAL*

"Miliband mobbed in Edinburgh" (angry scenes as Ed driven into shop) *NO*

"Cameron faces revolt over Scottish powers pledge" (Tory backbenchers don't like more powers for Scots) *YES*

OTHER: "Forces chiefs say indy leaves UK more vulnerable" *NO*

"EDF Concerns over INDY" *NO*

"Yes cars to get out vote" (Yes Scotland bankrolled cars for 300,000 first time voters) *YES*

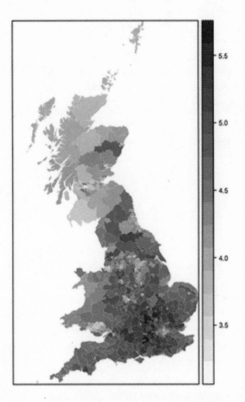

Appendice Two: This map shows the average public opinion on re-distribution of wealth for each British constituency. Lighter colours represent more economically left-wing thinking, those who agree with the statement 'Government should try to make incomes equal' while darker colours represent more economically right-wing think-ing, with those agreas agreeing more with the statement 'Govern-ment should be less concerned about equal incomes'. This illustrates the difference in political opinion between Scotland and England. Source: 'Constituency Opionion and Representation in Britain' by Nick Vivyan and Chris Hanretty 21/10/2014.

Appendice Three: A table showing the major parties' proposals to the Smith Commission regarding devolution of tax. Source: Smith Commission.

SHOULD THIS TAX BE DEVOLVED?

Key: Yes ✓ Partial/Caveats ~ No ✗

	Conservative	Lib Dem	Labour	SNP	Scottish Greens
INCOME TAX	✓	✓	~	✓	✓
INHERITANCE TAX	✗	✓	✗	✓	✓
CAPITAL GAINS TAX	✗	✓	✗	✓	✓
NATIONAL INSURANCE CONTRIBUTIONS	✗	✗	✗	✓	✓
AIR PASSENGER DUTY	✓	✓	✗	✓	✓
CORPORATION TAX	✗	✗	✗	✓	~
VALUE ADDED TAX	~	✗	✗	~	~
EXCISE DUTIES	✗	✗	✗	~	✓
WEALTH TAXES	✗	✗	✗	✓	✓
AGGREGATES LEVY	✗	✓	✗	✓	✓
BUSINESS RATE	✗	~	✗	✓	✓

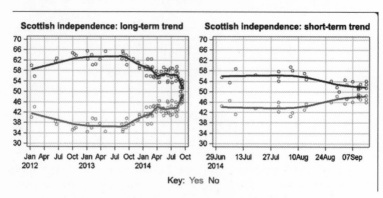

Scottish independence: long-term trend

Scottish independence: short-term trend

Jan Apr Jul Oct Jan Apr Jul Oct Jan Apr Jul Oct
2012 2013 2014

29Jun 13Jul 27Jul 10Aug 24Aug 07Sep
2014

Key: Yes No

Appendice Four: Independence Referendum Poll Tracker from January 2012 to October 2014. Source: Crikey.com.au.

Appendice Five: These exit polls were conduced on September 18th and 19th of September concerning the Indy Ref vote. Source: Lord Ashcroft Polls.

POST-REFERENDUM SCOTLAND POLL
18-19 SEPTEMBER 2014

1. How did you vote in the referendum?

%	ALL	Men	Women	AGE						2010 WESTMINSTER VOTE			
				16-24	25-34	35-44	45-54	55-64	65+	Con	Lab	SNP	LD
YES	45	47	44	51	59	53	52	43	27	5	37	86	39
NO	55	53	56	49	41	47	48	57	73	95	63	14	61

2. When did you finally make up your mind how to vote in the referendum?

%	YES voters		NO voters	
On referendum day	8		3	
In the last few days	7		3	
In the last week	6	52	3	28
In the last month	18		10	
Since the beginning of the year	13		9	
Longer ago than a year	10	48	10	72
I have always known how I would vote	38		62	

3. What were the two or three most important issues in deciding how you ultimately voted?

% naming among reasons	YES voters	NO voters	Men	Women
The NHS	54	36	39	50
The pound	7	57	35	34
Jobs	18	21	20	19
Prices	3	13	8	9
Disaffection with Westminster politics	74	4	38	33
Pensions	10	37	23	26
Defence & security	16	29	24	22
Benefits	13	7	9	11
Oil	20	6	13	12
Tax & public spending	33	32	35	31
EU membership	12	15	16	12
None of the above	4	7	5	6

2,047 adults who voted in the referendum were interviewed online (831) or by telephone (1,216) on 18 and 19 September 2014. Full data tables are available at www.LordAshcroftPolls.com

4. Would you be reluctant in any way to tell your friends, family or colleagues how you voted?

	YES voters	NO voters
Yes I would	11	14
No I would not	89	86

5. I am going to read out three reasons people have given for voting YES. Please can you rank them in order of how important they were in your decision, even if there were other reasons that were important to you? [All those who voted YES]

% saying 'most important reason'	YES voters
The principle that all decisions about Scotland should be taken in Scotland	70
That on balance Scotland's future looked brighter as an independent country	20
That independence would mean no more Conservative governments	10

6. I am going to read out three reasons people have given for voting NO. Please can you rank them in order of how important they were in your decision, even if there were other reasons that were important to you? [All those who voted NO]

% saying 'most important reason'	NO voters
The risks of becoming independent looked too great when it came to things like the currency, EU membership, the economy, jobs and prices	47
A strong attachment to the UK and its shared history, culture and traditions	27
A NO vote would still mean extra powers for the Scottish Parliament together with the security of remaining part of the UK, giving the best of both worlds	25

7. If it turns out that a majority has voted NO in the referendum, for how long do you think the question of whether Scotland should be independent or remain in the UK will remain settled?

%	YES voters	NO voters
For the next five years	45	20
For the next ten years	16	18
For the next generation	18	28
Forever	12	25
Don't know	9	8

ABOUT THE AUTHOR

Iain Macwhirter is an award-winning political commentator for the *Sunday Herald* and *The Herald*. Iain started at the BBC as a researcher after graduating from Edinburgh University, and became the BBC's Scottish Political Correspondent in 1987. In 1990 he moved to London to present political programmes for BBC network television such as 'Westminster Live' and 'Scrutiny'. He was a member of the Westminster Lobby for nearly ten years and columnist for a number of national newspapers including *The Observer* and *The Scotsman*. In 1999 he returned to Scotland to help launch the *Sunday Herald* and to present the BBC's 'Holyrood Live' TV programmes. He was also Rector of Edinburgh University 2009-11. In a co-production with STV in 2013, Iain presented a three-part history of Scottish Nationalism, *Road to Referendum*. *Disunited Kingdom* is his second book; it follows *Road to Referendum* (2013/2014).

PRAISE FOR *ROAD TO REFERENDUM*

"A truly important book, particularly at this moment. It offers a huge sweep of history and deals with recent Scottish politics in formidable, but never tedious detail."

Andrew Marr, BBC

"A terrific book. Macwhirter covers much more than he does in his TV documentary, and the book combines a broad history of Scotland's relationship with England from the time of Robert the Bruce onwards with a detailed analysis of the rise of the SNP, the creation of the Scottish parliament and the run-up to the referendum. It's a heavyweight, serious book, but it's a pleasure to read and it's full of shrewd insights. I'd recommend it highly."

Andrew Sparrow, *The Guardian*

"Iain Macwhirter is shrewd, insightful and with few rivals in the business of understanding – and explaining – the changing politics of Scotland."

Jonathan Freedland, *The Guardian*

"Iain Macwhirter offers a highly readable and personal account of Scottish history drawing on wide reading and a career during which he has followed these debates more closely and consistently than any other journalist. He enlivens old stories with new perspectives, challenges established wisdom and raises awkward questions for protagonists and antagonists in equal measure on either side of today's debate."

Professor James Mitchell, University of Edinburgh

"Iain Macwhirter's Road to Referendum is easily the most accessible piece of writing concerned with the independence debate. Not only one of the shrewdest commentaries on Scottish politics, it is also an important tribute to the country's history."

The List

"Peppered with typical Macwhirter one-liners... They could provide student essay questions for years to come with only the word "discuss" added to them."

Professor Tom Devine, *The Herald*

Disunited Kingdom:
How Westminster Won A Referendum But Lost Scotland
Iain Macwhirter
First Published by Cargo Publishing in 2014
SC376700
© Iain Macwhirter 2014

ISBN 978-1-908885-26-5

Printed & Bound by MBM Print SCS Ltd, Glasgow
Cover design by Craig Lamont
www.cargopublishing.com

Also available as:
Kindle Ebook
EPUB Ebook

MIX
Paper from
responsible sources
FSC® C117931